D0885329

In
Search
of
Wings

BOSTON BAPTIST COLLEGE LIBRARY
950 Metropolitan Avenue
Boston, MA 02136
Tel (617) 364-3510

In
Search
of
Wings

A Journey Back From Traumatic Brain Injury

By Beverley Bryant

Published by **WINGS**
South Paris, Maine

BOSTON BAPTIST COLLEGE LIBRARY
350 Metropolitan Ave.
Boston, MA 02136
Tel (617) 364-3510

IN SEARCH OF WINGS

Published by
WINGS
South Paris, Maine

Copyright © 1992 by Beverley Bryant
All Rights Reserved.

No part of this book may be reproduced in any form or transmitted by any electronically or mechanical means, including photocopying, recording or by any information storage and retrieval systems, without permission in writing from the author. Exceptions will be granted for reviewers who may quote brief passages for reviews in newspapers, other periodicals and broadcasts. Written requests for permission are welcomed, to be sent to the Publisher, 1 Clifford Court, So. Paris, Maine 04281

First Edition 1992
Printed in the United State of America

Cover Photo Courtesy ©1990 by Paule French. All Rights Reserved
Other Photographs by Peter Raymond
Design and Production by Julie Motherwell
ISBN 1-882332-00-8

Dedication

I dedicate the STRUGGLE to all the staff at the New England Rehabilitation Hospital in Portland, Maine, who worked with me and shared the laughter and shared the tears.

They found me wherever I was, and returned me safely to wherever I belonged. They showed me they cared, by being not only rebuilders, but the vehicle for my journey in search of wings.

I remember especially and want to thank *Trisha Allen* and *Sarah Bronson*, who shared the excitement of my physical therapy and the fear of never knowing what I would do next. We made it! *Dr. Rita Oliverio*, for her concern and always taking the time to listen, hear and be there; *Dr. David Marks*, for his expertise in dealing with my deficits and helping me cope; *Dr. G. T. Caldwell*, for his patience and time, and lectures when I needed them; *Elaine McMahon*, for the smile every day all day; *Julie Waterman*, in occupational therapy, for all the hours of work and special encouragement; *Carolyn Foley,* for just being my friend; and all *The Second Floor Staff* who watched over me, *Brenda, Barbara, Sandy, Sharon, Linda, George, Roland, Karen, Lisa, Mary-Ellen, Lori, TW, Dottie, Lorraine, June, Marci, Cynthia, Mary, Nancy, Paula, Suzette, George,* and *Gene* and any I've left out. Thanks for all the days and nights that you survived, smiling and still with a sense of humor. You're the greatest.

I dedicate the JOURNEY to *Kathy Kaczor,* who labored as my speech therapist for 15 months, travelled the road with me, and guided me back carefully and thoroughly. I thank you for helping me find the way, and when finding the way was impossible, for teaching me the strategies to compensate.

I dedicate the RETURN to *Donna and Tony Levesque.* Donna, a nurse in the head injury program, worked so hard and persevered with me in the hospital, and became a special personal friend as well. As a survivor herself, she had the knowledge the journey needs. She not only planted the seed for writing this book, but sustained it with love, caring and support along the way. Tony, a lab technician, made me laugh and find my sense of humor again. Without their friendship and encouragement, I would never have set out in search of wings.

I **dedicate the LOVE to my husband, *Gordon*,** for 30 years of love, caring and support. When your best friend and lover is at your side, all things are possible.

The journey back from T.B.I. is long and needs much nurturing en route. I thank you for all the love, the comfort, your patience with my deficits, your encouragement to go public with my book, and your guidance and help along the way.

I LOVE YOU.

THIS ONE'S FOR YOU!

Table of Contents

Introduction

PART I   To Start A Journey

Chapter 1......Soaring........................ 2

Chapter 2......Landings..................... 11

Chapter 3......Idle...ings 19

Chapter 4......Recharging 27

Chapter 5......Crashing 32

PART II   A Time To Rest

Chapter 6......Systems Check 40

Chapter 7......Overhaul..................... 45

Chapter 8......Fasten Seat Belts..... 60

Chapter 9......Discoveries................ 66

Chapter 10....Taking Off 71

Chapter 11....Water Courses 80

Chapter 12....Radio Check 85

Chapter 13....Proper Procedure ... 90

Chapter 14....Cockpit Changes 93

Chapter 15....Charity Flight 101

Chapter 16....OnThe Runway 109

Chapter 17....Ground School 117

Chapter 18....Pilot's Log 125

Table of Contents

Part III A Space To Fly

Chapter 19 .... Introduction to Soloing 130

Chapter 20 .... Navigating 137

Chapter 21 .... Soloing 143

Chapter 22 .... Ignition 151

Chapter 23 .... Trusting The Wind 157

Chapter 24 .... Accelerating 170

Chapter 25 .... Cleared For Takeoff 184

Chapter 26 .... Co-Piloting 195

Chapter 27 .... Roger, Tower 210

Chapter 28 .... Reconnoitering 216

Chapter 29 .... Flaps Up! 221

Chapter 30 .... Toward The Unknown 228

Introduction

Most people have never heard of Traumatic Brain Injury. I know I hadn't. Then one day it slipped into my life, like the thief it is. I never saw it coming.

Traumatic Brain Injury can be described as an injury to the brain that is caused by external forces. It is not caused by illness or aging. It often produces a diminished or altered state of consciousness, which results in temporary or permanent impairment of cognitive abilities or physical functioning. It may result in the disturbance of behavioral or emotional functioning. It may also cause partial or total functional disability, or psychosocial maladjustment.

No one expects that T.B.I. will ever happen to them. Other medical conditions have been dramatized and advertised. There aren't many people who haven't in some way been affected, made aware, or warned of cancer and its implications. Muscular dystrophy, multiple sclerosis, cystic fibrosis, AIDS, heart disease, etc. are all discussed openly and we know of their devastation. We are constantly made aware that one out of every so many families will become affected. No one ever thinks that they are going to be disabled with a head injury....and yet, more people in America today are suffering from head injury than any of the above.

My journey in search of wings is one that many others have taken before me and a journey that too many others will follow. It is an experience that no one should have to take. I've asked myself over and over again. Why Me? But WHY doesn't matter very much. The fact is, it could happen to anybody at anytime.

There is no cure, only prevention. In order to prevent it, we must be made aware. When head injury strikes, it is with the speed of lightning. Its effects go on for a very long time, often forever.

Sometimes, there is no survivor.

Sometimes, the devastating physical effects are very obvious. Sometimes, you cannot see or find the myriad of deficits, for they lie hidden within a web of normalcy.

All types of head injury hurt, and change with time. Survivors need to be, not only aware, but convinced of that.

I am a survivor, and hopefully, by releasing, sharing and recovering part of myself, it will help in diagnosis, understanding and acceptance of traumatic brain injury.

Much of this book has been written by piecing together entries in my *memory book* during that time. As a cross reference to incidents, I used my medical records, my daily notes, and my family and nurses' corroboration for accuracy.

The poetry readings, *remnants*, were personal thoughts and feelings I was never able to express or tell anyone at the time, but I remember them well. Sometimes, in the retelling, I have made them humorous. Looking back now, they were. At the time; however, there was no laughter.

Nothing about brain injury is funny. Nor are the effects to be taken lightly. I have to laugh at my own experiences, or I would cry forever for what I have lost.

By reading **IN SEARCH OF WINGS**, the medical specialists, professionals, nurses, therapists, and the head injury teams will know that their work is needed and appreciated, even if their patients are unable to tell them.

Hopefully, by sharing **IN SEARCH OF WINGS**, the families who deal with survivors on a day-to-day basis will see that we love them and are trying to do the best we can. It is hard for all of us, especially them.

Hopefully, by writing **IN SEARCH OF WINGS**, it will release me from some of the haunting memories of the past, the constant fear of reoccurrence, and the anger I still feel for the me that's left. For the survivor, it is a constant struggle.

Those who are far enough along in their own trek can read it and recognize that the fear, anger, hope, and frustrations they are experiencing are all part of the recovery process.

Most of all, that while they struggle silently in search of wings, they are not now, nor will ever be, alone.

Remnants

Remnants (poetry interspersed within the chapters) were my innermost thoughts I was unable to share with anyone, for a long time.

People with head injury may never get a chance to talk about what they remember, or what they endured. Their family and friends may never understand how the mending process leaves their loved one with remnants of memories; some good and some, maybe not so good.

Some survivors are angry and some are lost in their own world. Some are struggling silently to find themselves; while many others, undiagnosed, walk our streets and don't understand what has happened to them. They may read pieces or remnants and, maybe, recognize themselves.

For those who cannot write or remember, I hope remnants will speak for them...and it will help the hurt go away.

In Search Of Wings

At birth, I start a journey
to build my roots and things.
When my pathway's interrupted
I start to search for wings

I have the knowledge deep inside
and all the strength it brings,
to climb above the obstacles
that impede my search for wings.

Nothing stops the human spirit
when it decides to soar.
It just needs a time to rest
and space to fly once more.

To Start A Journey

CHAPTER ONE

Soaring

Like many nights before, I was driving my sports car home from a gymnastics meet. Being a National Gymnastics Judge, I was in the middle of a very busy season and was accustomed to driving all hours of the day and night in my job of judging. I thoroughly enjoyed my work.

Little did I know then, I was about to become another head injury statistic.

I had spent the day at a meet, judging beginners who tumbled, danced and waited nervously for my evaluation. Although my credentials allow me to judge at the advanced levels of gymnastic competitions, my true love is judging the younger beginning gymnasts who are just getting started. I love the beguiling smiles they give before they begin their routine, and the honesty with which they finish. Enjoying the little ones, who have not yet lost their innocence to the *thrill of victory and the agony of defeat* is much like enjoying a parfait dessert after a roast beef and potato dinner. During the past few years, I've enjoyed judging in Oregon, Vermont, Nevada, Massachusetts, Wisconsin, Rhode Island, California, New Hampshire, Indiana, and New York. I'd judged National Collegiate Championships and the International Special Olympics. Yet, to come home and judge the Maine youngsters is what I really loved.

I had spent the day judging at a private gymnastics club in Biddeford, about 75 miles from my home. I had driven south to the City of Auburn in the morning and car-pooled the rest of the way with Joyce D'Augustine, my friend and colleague. We arrived back at her home about 10 p.m. that evening. A storm had been forecast. It was cold and the temperature was right at freezing. There were two routes I could take to get home. One way was a better road, but it was quite a bit longer. I decided to take the shorter route and travel the 20 miles before experiencing any bad driving conditions. I fastened my seat belt, and as my car stuttered and stammered trying frantically to warm up, I reassured Joyce that I would be back at 5:30 in the morning to pick her up. We had to be in Yarmouth at 7:00 a.m. to prepare for and judge at the Annual Maine Judges' Cup Competition the next day.

Before I had gone a mile on the back road, the storm arrived, fast and furious. God! How the snow fell. It enveloped everything so quickly. Only if you lived in the Oxford Hills region, could you understand the instant change in the weather.

The darkness of the night on February 23, 1990, was like most other nights; moving over the day quickly like a blanket, sliding in and blocking out the sunlight. Little did I know then, that I wasn't coming home from the journey. I was about to enter a world that I never knew existed. It would be a long time before that sun would reappear, and my life would ever again be the same.

All of a sudden, on a slippery curve on the back road, the car slid out from under me. I tried to avoid blinding lights that appeared in front of me and experienced a feeling of flying. My car (according to the driver of a car behind me) spun out of control, accelerated, flew over a huge snowbank, and landed crooked so that my side was buried under the snow. I'm told the rescue squad dug me out and rushed me to Stephens Memorial Hospital in Norway, Maine, where I was admitted for closed head injury. I don't remember the trip, being treated in the Emergency Room, or being admitted to the hospital. I did have a dreamy recollection of trying to get my seatbelt off.

The ME Before

My life and past for the time being became only shattered remnants, forgotten and confused. They were such strong and vivid memories, too.

Gordon was my wonderful husband and best friend. We resided in South Paris, a small rural town in southwestern Maine for the past seventeen years. We had three sensitive, loving and independent children, each finishing college to become a professional. Mark was a Supervisor of Project and Quality Management with AT&T in the United Kingdom. Kimberly was a lead Nuclear Engineer at the Naval Base in Kittery, Maine. Carrie was a first-grade teacher in the neighboring town of East Sumner. We were fortunate and lucky to have been able to share their lives with all of them.

We also had two delightfully robust and inquisitive grandsons. Our lives had been full of growth, challenge, travel, excitement, enjoyment, and rewards.

When our nest emptied, we found other challenges to follow and other things to do; things that we had not had the time to delve into before, with children.

Our family had always been very close knit, though we each had pursued individual careers.

Gordon had just retired as Assistant Superintendent of Schools in the Oxford Hills School District after thirty years in public education, twenty of which had been in school administration.

Having a Master's Degree in Education, I taught physical education for 13 years in New York, Rhode Island, and Maine. I had served on several Accreditation Committees for Secondary Schools and for many years was a critic teacher for student teachers in my field.

I'd coached 13 different varsity sports and produced and directed eight different dance productions. Different things and the search for new knowledge excited me. I loved change and thrived in seeking it out.

When we returned to Maine from Rhode Island, our children were approaching the teenage years. I wanted to be home with them. I felt this was a time I wanted to be there, if they needed help. Though I loved teaching, I never returned. There were no regrets either, I had a ball enjoying my own children.

For 15 years, I'd been a member of the Southern Maine craftsmen and created patterns for numerous stuffed toys and animals for the Bryant Limited Zoo, my own crafts business.

I retired three years ago, after 13 years as the State Judging Director for the sport of gymnastics. I wanted to spend less time behind my desk and more, out actually judging.

I also wanted to spend more time with my husband in our own rental business. Gordon and I had purchased eight apartment buildings (just before the Maine real estate market skyrocketed) to secure a retirement investment for our future. It was a big gamble, but we read all the *No Money Down* books and decided to just "go for it." I became the planner, bookkeeper and analyst for our financial future. Gordon became the renovator, repairman and contractor. He loved his new hands-on challenge and I loved my part of the adventure.

So that we could better understand our own real estate investments, we both studied and became real estate brokers in the Oxford Hills area. We enjoyed meeting and working directly with people.

I raced through the GRI (Graduate Realtor Institute) three levels in one year and had tested and earned my Level 3 designation, one week before my accident.

I loved the challenge of learning new things. The more I scheduled myself to do in a time frame, the better I performed. I worked best under pressure and when the going got tough, I produced. I learned quickly. Tell me once and I rarely ever forgot. Show me once and it was ingrained forever. I gave clinics for my colleagues on effective ways to study, learn and retain.

Why am I telling you all this? So that you can understand what kind of a life I led, and the happiness around which my life evolved and the satisfaction that permeated my world of work.

I was totally contented, inspired by anything new and loved being with people. I was well known to my colleagues as a leader who was calm in the face of adversity and was a mediator for those who weren't. I love others. I loved my own life and everything about it.

A Time When

There was a time when I believed
There's nothing I can't do.
A time when I'd do anything,
That someone asked me to.

My folks made sure that I grew up
Believing in myself.
Life was what I made of it,
And not left on the shelf.

What you want is not a dream.
It's what you work to make it.
If you cannot reach that star,
Then carve a step and take it.

So all my life, I grew to find
That what they said was true.
I accomplished everything
That I set out to do.

A time when I had many plans
To venture for and wide...
To search each nook and cranny
And reap the dreams inside.

Bit life cuts short too many dreams
And truth gets in the way.
In one "cold and crashing" moment
I became the ME today.

CHAPTER   TWO

 # Landings

I didn't remember anything until the next morning. I was disoriented, confused and unable to think. The back of my head hurt, but more of a dull soreness than a sharp pain. I was nauseous and felt like I had been run over by a truck. My accident happened on a Friday night. When the admitting surgeon, Dr. Story, arrived Saturday morning, I knew immediately I had to trust him, although I had never met him before.

I was unable to think rationally, but I felt confident he would make any necessary decisions for me. I think I even asked him to. My brain was jumbled and I wanted to avoid lights, noise and just sleep. I learned very quickly that they don't let

Landing

people who have sustained head injury sleep. Dr. Story came in my room often, asking me questions and checking on me. He wanted to know my phone number, but I couldn't remember it. I tried each time he came in and when he left, I had already forgotten what he had asked. Then he would return and ask me again. I finally asked a nurse if she could find my phone number. I'm sure she looked it up in the telephone book for me and wrote it down on a 3x5 card. I practiced reading it over and over. When Dr. Story came back the next time to ask me, I tried to remember it, but it was useless. I looked down at the card and read it off. I'm sure that he knew I was reading it, but it really didn't matter. Unknown to me, I had just learned my first of many strategies I would use in the months ahead.

I had never been in a position where I was totally unable to help myself. It was very important for me to know that I could trust my doctor, because I couldn't think for myself.

I had a feeling that I was supposed to be somewhere for a meet. It was Saturday and I always had a gymnastics meet on Saturday. I knew I had to get out of here. But for a while, I forgot about doing anything except resting and trying not to think. I would just have to trust Dr. Story until I could trust myself again.

The weekend passed. On Monday morning my regular doctor, Dr. Ware, returned and made his rounds. He was surprised to find me as a patient. During our conversation, he asked me casually when Dr. Story was going to send me home. Obviously, I didn't know, but his question made me suddenly realize that I didn't know where my home was. I knew what it looked like and what everything in it looked like, but I had no idea how to get there.

I suddenly realized I would have a problem if they released me. I couldn't find my way home.

Dr. Ware returned a short time later to run some tests and told me that I couldn't go home, for a few days at least. I felt relief. In the meantime, maybe I could figure out where I lived.

I know somewhere I have a home
That may be ours, but where?
I see the house and furnishings,
But the road to it's not there.

You need to show me where it is?
And then I wouldn't mind it.
But right now, I cannot think.
Tomorrow I will find it.

A head injury prevents an individual from making rational decisions, or understanding what is happening. Consistency is imperative and any change becomes a conflict. I knew that I needed Dr. Story to stay nearby, I trusted him to do what was right. My husband understood and assured me he would see to it that Dr. Story remained in charge of my care. I rested easier.

Even though I had much respect for Dr. Ware, who had been my physician for over 10 years, I could not deal with change. Dr. Ware remained on my case as a consultant. Dr. Story continued as my doctor.

I had difficulty understanding time. My daughter was standing by my bed one day, when Dr. Story came in. He asked me to tell him the day, date and month. Apparently, I gave him the wrong everything.

After he had left the room, my daughter said, "Gee Mom! You just had to look over his head, there's a calendar there." My eyes scanned the board and I found the calendar on my wall. While I recognized it as being a calendar, I remember lying there trying to figure out how I was supposed to use it.

Doctors thought I had contusions of the brainstem and possibly the cerebellum. I continued to have difficulty walking. My diagnostic tests were negative or inconclusive, I was assured that it was just a matter of time until I recovered. I received excellent daily care and improved as the days passed.

Only 18 months before, I had undergone surgery for a herniated spinal disc that had calcified and cut off a spinal nerve. While the surgery was extremely successful in relieving me of the physical pain, I had procrastinated much too long before seeing the neurosurgeon. As a result, I had suffered permanent nerve damage in my right leg and foot. I now seemed to have a lot of trouble controlling my right leg. That was another obstacle in becoming steadier on my feet. But, I felt more confident with each day.

However, once the I.V.'s were removed, the staff realized I wasn't eating or drinking. It wasn't a conscious decision. I wasn't even aware of it. This was a new problem for me. I loved food. Suddenly, I found that I didn't eat. It wasn't because I didn't want to. Each time my meal came, I intended to eat. But for some reason, I never did. It was almost as though I forgot it was there, once it arrived.

After a couple of days, both doctors expressed concern and asked me why I wasn't eating or drinking. I didn't know. I had difficulty even remembering that I wasn't. I certainly couldn't understand why I didn't. I told Dr. Ware that I had a feeling I was unable to make a decision of what to eat on my tray. I was hungry. I told him I thought if they put only one item on my tray, I would eat it. It didn't particularly matter what it was. He smiled and said he knew just the thing. When lunch came, the tray was full. I didn't eat.

That evening, Dr. Story walked into my room unexpectedly and found me crying. He pulled up a chair and tried to comfort me. I hardly ever cried and I was embarrassed to be caught in this rare occurrence. He was relieved to learn I was not in pain. I remember confiding in him how I was concerned I didn't eat. I always planned to, but when my food came, I didn't. The stupidity of the predicament was absurd to even me. It must have seemed completely ludicrous to him. But he dried my tears and told me not to think about it. I did not know then that it was part of my head injury.

As the days passed though, everyone grew concerned. The problem of not eating or drinking produced no voiding. I was told I was in danger of my systems shutting down if I didn't eat. I knew they were very concerned, but I was still unable to do anything about it.

During his visits, Dr. Ware took it more lightly. I resorted to joking about it with him. I needed to cover up the fact that I was unable to cope with the problem.

My doctors then became involved in a professional difference of opinion regarding my course of treatment. Dr. Ware wanted to send me home to recuperate. Dr. Story wanted to send me to a rehabilitation hospital.

When Dr. Ware told me of Dr. Story's intentions, I was still unable to deal with my own health problem; much less conflict between two people I trusted to make my decisions.

I told Gordon I was unable to deal with this and asked him to get me out of the hospital immediately. The problem, however, became moot. By then, for some unknown reason, I had begun to eat and drink. There was still some time to pass before I was able to void. When I finally did, Dr. Story gave me the OK to go home. I had been in the hospital for two weeks.

Dr. Story advised me not to return to work or drive, until he said so. I never did take advice too well, especially when I really wanted something bad enough. I felt my head had fully recovered and I just needed to get out and do things.

I felt capable and raring to go again after my long rest. I could only be held down just so long. I had things to do and places to go.

CHAPTER   THREE

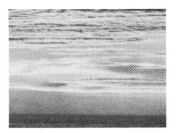

Idle...ings...

I knew I wanted to get back into the swing of
things as quickly as possible, once free of the
restrictions of the hospital. In 14 years of judging,
I had never had to break a contract and I certainly
wasn't about to start. I felt sitting at home was not
what I needed.

Gordon did not agree, but knew that voicing
his objections would be worse. So just two days
after my release from the hospital, I arrived at the
State High School Gymnastics Championships to
fulfill my contract as the head judge on floor
exercise.

I found areas that suddenly became problems
for me; ones that only a couple of weeks ago had

been my best strengths. I knew the knowledge was still there. I had to try to believe that whatever was affecting my head wouldn't interfere with my judging ability.

However, I also knew that I could not let these gymnasts down. I could not let my pride overshadow fair and accurate judging for these kids who had worked so hard. I took every precaution, in case I was unable to do the job. I prepared a procedure for the alternate judge to take over after the first performance, if I felt or she felt that I wasn't doing an accurate job.

As usual, the meet director had put my table on the side of the mat where I could see the whole gym. In the past, I judged very quickly. I usually finished computing my score for each competitor before the other judges. While waiting for other scores, I had always enjoyed watching what was going on in the other events. It also allowed me to keep an eye on the total meet; I was usually the senior judge present.

It was well known among the different coaches that I preferred this table arrangement.

This time, however, as I tried to watch the gymnasts do their tumbling runs in warmup, I could very quickly see that I was unable to keep my eyes focused on the gymnast. I found my eyes wandering to the other events in the middle of her run. Getting my attention back to the gymnast I was supposed to be watching, was almost impossible. Recognizing this would be a problem later, I had to immediately figure a way to compensate. I did it by having the meet director move my table around to the other side of the mat, so that I was facing a blank wall. It surprised all of my colleagues, but it worked.

Another strange thing occurred. After the gymnast acknowledged me at the end of her performance, I looked down to begin to compute her score. The only recollection of her routine I had was what I had written on my worksheet.

I couldn't replay her routine again in my brain like before.

A judge mentally replays a routine as she reads her notes and calculates her execution deductions. Everything this gymnast did was written in front of me, but I could not remember it being performed.

As a judge, I was known for being able to tell you the 34th girl's third tumbling series on a given date, and what she did wrong.

I knew I had a problem.

Somehow, I was able to function without anyone else becoming aware or noticing. That was important to me. I didn't want anyone else to know I was having difficulty.

I did my job by making slight adjustments. I worked differently and slower, but I still trusted my accuracy. I just had to be certain that every movement the gymnast made during her routine was recorded on my paper.

Doctors had told me (and I believed) that my deficits were a temporary nuisance and would shortly go away. I was sure it was only a matter of time and I would be fine. No one ever explained to me the most important and vital information; I had a head injury and the effects were not going to go away for a long time.

At my followup visits, the doctors asked me if I was still having any problems. I tried to explain what I had experienced during judging; that as a routine was being performed, I made notes accordingly. My memory of a routine was verified by these notes. Thus, I knew which segments occurred when, because they were written down in black and white in front of me. But now, my memory was no longer in sync with what I saw recorded on paper. I identified this as a problem that had just appeared.

I thought having this information would help them figure out what was wrong.

My doctors expressed surprise that there were things I still couldn't do. They felt I should have fully recovered by now. I agreed that the deficits weren't that important. As long as they didn't make me non-functional, I wasn't overly concerned. I knew I still wasn't back to normal, but I was able to hide it from others.

I thought maybe I just had to really believe I could do everything and I would be able to. So I decided to believe I could do anything - mind over matter! Unfortunately, Traumatic Brain Injury (T.B.I.) doesn't work that way. Cause and Effect become separate and non-connected.

When I told the doctors I was ready to resume driving, they were suddenly hesitant. They had not been so worried about any of my other deficits, but suggested I wait for a while to drive.

I didn't understand and became very frustrated and confused.

Deficits are very real. Deficits are conflicts that need to be dealt with, not ignored. Time does not heal these wounds. If a patient with a head injury, or the doctor, is lucky enough to be able to identify specific deficits, they need to work together to correct them as soon as possible.

I learned too late that time is not always the sure healer it's made out to be.

Many people, after a brain injury, will not realize they are different. Others will not accept that they are different. I never wanted to discuss what I was finding difficult to do or accept it as real. Since no one really knew what to do to correct it, or why my deficits hadn't disappeared, I felt I had to beat this problem alone.

I wasn't about to tell my friends. I couldn't very well tell my colleagues. They wouldn't understand. I didn't understand what was happening myself. How could they?

I certainly didn't know why. But I knew that all of a sudden, I was different...VERY different! I was the one who had to live with this, but I wanted somebody to find out what was happening to me.

Why was I finding truth in the *out of sight, out of mind* theory? I could not remember what someone had just said or did. Why did I begin to operate on a "one track" system and seemingly overnight have trouble with switching tasks?

I found I had trouble staying tuned in to any lengthy conversations. When my daughter, Carrie, would stop after school and begin to tell me about her day in the classroom, I would find myself drifting off and not able to concentrate on what she was saying. I knew she wondered why I was no longer as interested in her day as I had been. I used to be her best listener. But now, for some reason, I was unable to stay tuned in. I began to try harder to pay attention, but it was almost impossible. She became hurt and I became angry.

I don't, and never did, like "idling".

I WANT IT NOW

There was a time, I did it all.
I stooped so low. I stood so tall.

I worked like ten. I played the best.
I knew the rules. I passed the test.

I cast the roles. I played the star.
I wrote the scripts. I drove a car.

I did the things, that made me ME.
There was nothing left, I couldn't be.

Things were always what they seemed.
Life was always as I dreamed.

What happened first, I can't recall,
But in one skid, I lost it all.

I need some help, to stay on track.
I need that help to get it back.

I remember when, this wasn't true.
I used to go. I loved to do.

But now I wait, for things to change.
This needing help is all too strange.

I want to leave, yet I can't go.
I want it fast. I get it slow.

I see it slow. I dream it fast.
I always know that it won't last.

I live the past from day to day.
I don't know where mine went away.

I'm not that one, I used to be.
Just be assured, this isn't me!

I don't know when. I don't care how.
I had it then. I want it now.

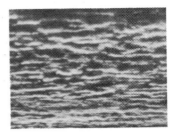

CHAPTER FOUR

Recharging

Although I knew my deficits remained while judging, I worked around them. For the first time ever, I gladly ended my season early.

I used some flight mileage I had accumulated from my gymnastics activities, for two free tickets to Australia with a stopover in Hawaii. At that point, it sounded exciting to both Gordon and me. We arranged to have this long vacation together during the months of May and early June.

The year so far had been a trying one and we wanted to take some time to enjoy each other. We had always been the best of friends. I was ready for a quiet, less confusing atmosphere where I didn't have to be in the public eye every day, and Gordon could use some time away from tenant problems.

Other than a recurring, bothersome ear infection, I was experiencing no major problems. I had regained the strength in my hand and my leg had recovered as much as I could expect it to. I felt my deficits were diminishing and was looking forward to getting away. It was a restful trip that made no demands on me, and provided the opportunity to just enjoy without thinking or making decisions; a good time to rest. I knew that some things were still a problem for me, i.e., decisions and complex problems, but I tended to ignore them. I was looking forward to the chance to recharge so that I could begin to take off again.

Our trip was totally exciting. While in Hawaii, we laid on the beach at Waikiki, toured the island of Oahu, shopped, relaxed, and did the show circuit. We went on to Aukland, New Zealand, and Sydney, Australia, where we toured, took in everything and craved for more. It was wonderful. We flew to Cairns, and then travelled north to Port Douglas, where we snorkeled off the Great Barrier Reef and went reef fishing. We enjoyed the mountains, the aborigines, the kangaroos, and the koalas. The scenery and the peacefulness were magnificent.

Arriving home after a 21 hour flight, I stayed over in a hotel near the airport. The following morning I was to take a 7 a.m. flight to Lincoln, Nebraska, with the Maine High School Senior All-State Gymnastics Team. Gordon returned home to South Paris.

It didn't take me long to get moving again. My children had asked for pineapples from Hawaii. But since we had flown onto Sydney from Hawaii, pineapples were out of the question. I felt badly. When we walked into the airport in Lincoln, Nebraska, for our return flight to Maine, there were crates of Hawaiian pineapple. United was shipping them free on passenger flights for a cancer drive. I loaded up and returned home excited, with my arms full of Hawaiian pineapple for my family.

Once back home, I tried to spend more time out in the sun relaxing. I felt back to normal. I had resumed daytime driving, but had not driven at night yet.

In late June, I eagerly returned to my job as a realtor. But once back to work, I found that many normal parts of my job were hard for me to do. I had difficulty remembering the information on new listings. I had my husband do all my showings because I was unable to recall information I needed. I had difficulty staying with a task. I would tend to skip from one thing to another, even forgetting incoming phone calls I had taken. I avoided any new challenging work. It was obvious to me I was not the same person who, just a few months before, had passed the GRI Level 3.

I knew then, something was still wrong, but believed all I needed was just more time to readjust to my work environment. After all, I had not dealt with real estate since my accident and it was almost like a new job to me. I would take a little more time and no one else need know. So, I silently struggled to do the job better and be more careful in my work.

In July, there were occasions when I couldn't remember things that had just happened. I was only made aware of it, when someone else was with me, and would mention something related to what was either just said or just happened. I would have no idea what they were talking about because I seemed to have lost my immediate memory recall.

I remember distinctly one noon, my husband and I were having lunch. We were both listening to a radio broadcast pertaining to our school system and were very interested. I started toward the sink with a plate of spaghetti during a commercial. Next thing I knew, I was lying on the floor looking up at my husband .

I heard him say, " All right?"

I knew I had missed the first part of the sentence, "Are you ...?"

I said, "Yes."

But I noticed I was suddenly very tired, and wondered what had happened. Why didn't I hear the sentence? Why did I drop the plate?

I was frustrated and angry. I considered what happened only an isolated incident, a fluke. I was fine. My brain worked OK. I only needed to clean the spaghetti off the floor and walls.

CHAPTER FIVE

Crashing

Two weeks later on July 28, my parents arrived from central Florida to spend the month of August with us. I was looking forward to spending much time just relaxing and enjoying their company. It was a very hot day and I had spent most of the day swimming in our pool.

My husband came out to the patio and sat down in a chair. I swam over and encouraged him to come in and take a swim; it was so hot.

He looked at me and said, "Bev, I just got OUT!"

At first, I thought he was joking. Then I noticed under his chair was wet and water was dripping off his bathing suit. He said he had just been swimming and talking with me for at least ten minutes. Not only did I not remember, but I was positive he walked directly from the house to the chair and had immediately sat down.

That same evening, while at the home of my neighbor and good friend, I fell unconscious in the middle of a conversation. I was rushed to the hospital by ambulance.

When I awoke, my last remembrance was riding in the truck with my husband more than a mile to my neighbor's house and now, here I was in a hospital room. How did this happen? My records indicate I was admitted with either a stroke in the left brain or a seizure with Todd's Paralysis.

Immediately, I realized I couldn't move my right arm or leg. I knew right away that I was in more trouble than the last time I was here. It was my right side extremities, but this time, it seemed to be much worse.

I didn't know what had happened to me and that worried me most. Gordon and my parents had arrived. I could see they were deeply concerned. They kept saying everything would be all right, but it wasn't much consolation.

Within a couple of days, I realized the doctors weren't sure either.

My mother was sure it was a stroke. She had spent 30 years as a registered nurse. I prayed she was wrong, but I wanted to find out. Doctors couldn't confirm whether it was a seizure or a stroke. I wanted to know what was happening.

I think perhaps that was the hardest part, the most frustrating, the not knowing. I felt that any minute they would suddenly discover the problem, I would be cured and go home. Just 15 months before while hospitalized for my back surgery, I had spent four days in the cardiac unit at Central Maine Medical Center with a chest pain that took doctors five days to diagnose. It turned out to be a developing pneumothorax that required the insertion of a chest tube. I was sure this cure would be discovered suddenly too.

Down deep though, I faced the fact that whatever it was, it had struck when I least expected it. That made it the worst kind of whatever it was. I do not particularly like to be surprised. One day they'd think they'd found the cause, then the next day they'd think it was something else. Neurological diagnostic tests were negative.

I had no trouble eating this time. I knew that I had some of the same deficits as before. Physically, I was in worse shape. I was scared and depressed.

I knew I would have trouble formulating thoughts and processing information again. I tried to keep my answers as simple as I could, so no one would find out. I tried to hide the fact that my arm and leg didn't work right and said as little as possible. My arm began working again, although it remained very weak. I was determined to fix it this time myself. I regained some mobility during the two weeks I was in the hospital, but was still unsteady on my feet.

On the day I was to be discharged, Dr. Medd, my admitting physician at Stephens Memorial Hospital, was in my room giving me my final directions. The physical therapist walked in and asked if I was ready to go for a walk? Dr. Medd casually remarked that a walk would not be necessary, I was being discharged. The therapist appeared surprised, looked right at him and sternly said, "She's not going home."

I sat back on the bed to watch Dr. Medd who was one of the most prominent, well respected physicians at the hospital tell this physical therapist a thing or two.

Crashing

Much to my surprise, he turned to me and said, "Well, Beverley, I guess you are not going home."

I just stared in disbelief. It was then I realized that doctors and therapists work as team members. The physical therapist questioned my reality orientation. This would pave the way for what was to come.

The consensus of opinion then was that I should be referred to a rehabilitation hospital. I did not object. I wanted to find out what had happened to me, so I could prevent it from happening again.

A referral specialist from New England Rehabilitation Hospital arrived to review my records and examine me. Because the hospital's pre-admission committee was in session at the same time, I received a quick admittance.

Dr. Medd assured my husband that the rehabilitation hospital would be able to do more intricate and extensive testing. They would be able to get a clearer idea of what my problems were. They also would follow up with the proper, necessary rehabilitation. By this time, I was readily agreeable to this plan. I could not deal with waking up and suddenly, finding myself in a hospital again.

Dr. Medd assured me New England Rehabilitation Hospital would be a productive experience. He was absolutely right.

PART II

A Time To Rest

Rehab

If into each man God has given one will,
But he becomes injured and flouders until,
You try fifty ways on which recovery depends.
I have fifty more, my family defends.

Who will translate when we're finished and done.
Our one hundred attempts are no better than one.
But if into each patient, one hundred converge,
When he is made whole, one man will emerge.

CHAPTER SIX

Systems Check

A primary focus at New England Rehabilitation Hospital is head injury. My saga was a very familiar story to them. None of the problems and deficits I had encountered surprised them. The doctors there, assured me the latest hospitalization was secondary to the head injury I had received as a result of the accident. They seemed knowledgeable and prepared to deal with my situation.

Their diagnosis was that I had sustained *traumatic brain injury*, injury to the brain caused by an external blow and affecting cognitive, physical, behavioral, or emotional functioning. I had mild to moderate head injury but, unfortunately for me, my deficits were in areas that included reasoning and judgment.

I spent ten weeks as an in-patient in the head injury program. The stay was not to be easy for anyone. Specialized testing found deficits that had gone unnoticed since February.

I had a propriocepter problem in the brain which directly affected my arm and leg. This added complication to my old injury that had left me with severe nerve damage.

My sensory and strength tests measured 0-2 (on a scale of 0-5) on the right side. An EMG showed chronic denervation of the muscles in my right leg. I began an intensive physical therapy program to address these deficiencies. Because of my head injury, I found I needed to visually see a problem to understand how to correct it. I worked with mirrors and close supervision.

In Occupational therapy they had to use "blinders" to keep me focused and those were good for only about 10-20 seconds. I could hold a conversation or stay tuned in for no more than 12 seconds. I could not hold a writing utensil or write legibly. They made large grips for my pencils and pens. They braced my right wrist and hand so that I did not get my hand caught in the wheels of my wheelchair, or bend it the wrong way.

I couldn't remember where they would put items minutes after they told me. In Speech Therapy, they found I was unable to recall 3 numbers in a row. My information processing was considerably slowed. I could only understand simple sentences said slowly. I could not retain or recall verbal information. My memory functions were impaired. I was totally unable to concentrate and was distracted by any change or any sound in my environment.

The staff was amazed I had been able to get by this long, without others becoming aware of my deficits. The nursing staff became very concerned about my safety. I had become extremely impulsive. I believed I was able to walk and go anywhere by myself and usually tried. They made sure I was *grey-belted* (a restraint) into my wheelchair for my own safety at all times.

It took them less than 12 hours to decide I also needed a device, called a *wander guard*, which locked on my wrist and wheelchair to keep me in the area and away from the exit doors and elevators. The wander guard was similar to a watch and set off an alarm if it came within three feet of an exit.

There were things I didn't like and couldn't accept. I had always been free to do my own thing, make my own way, and I resented anything that restricted me. What was worse, I didn't understand what was happening or why it was necessary. Even though the medical staff was concerned and cooperative to my needs, I didn't think that I needed any special care; except I knew I was unsteady on my feet and couldn't walk alone.

I was so eager for them to find out what had happened to me, so that I could prevent it from happening again. Because of that, I tried hard. I struggled with little things, like trying to remember the therapists' names; continually forgetting that all I had to do was read their nametags.

I told what seemed like an endless number of different personnel what they wanted to know. How many stairs in my house? How many people in my family? Where my bedroom was located within the house? I knew these answers perfectly.

I was glad that they asked me easy ones. They realized my need to hear things slowly and carefully, so they took their time.

I can remember going through cognitive testing and struggling to figure out the answers. I expected them to find the solutions to my problems overnight; why I was having difficulty. Then, by magic, make them disappear.

For months, I had been trying to deal with things that gave me trouble. I told my doctors there were certain things I could no longer do, because I had no immediate memory recall. They couldn't understand and didn't seem to want to believe me. Yet, the New England Rehabilitation Hospital doctors and specialists were telling me there were many other things giving me trouble, and certain other things I could no longer do. I couldn't understand and didn't seem to want to believe them.

It is ironic how often we are forced to listen and yet, are incapable of hearing.

CHAPTER SEVEN

Overhaul

As I worked my way through testing in different therapy areas, I met up with so many things I had trouble doing.

At first, I didn't know that I had become deficient in physical and mental areas and was literally, at the mercy of the professionals into whose care I was entrusted. They knew what they had to do. But, I didn't.

My job was to cooperate and try to do whatever they wanted me to. One of my irritating obstacles was time. I always wanted to work longer than my scheduled therapy sessions.

Admitting and accepting my condition was another matter. I firmly believed that I could do many things that the therapists knew I couldn't. They spent weeks trying to convince me to slow down in my attempt to try them. I was willing to try anything, and usually before I had given it any thought.

I could not see day-to-day progress. Though gradually as the weeks passed, I began to notice changes. Very slowly I began to realize that these people who were strangers to me, were asking for my trust and knew how to help me. I only had to join the inevitable challenge and let them.

Letting them was the most difficult.

Mental Storage

It is not the pen or pencil
That enables us to be.
Nor is the ability to grasp them,
The part that holds the key.

Each alone is not enough.
It takes more to suffice.
For all the work that they must do,
The brain must do it twice.

So when our head's in disrepair,
All the contents change it.
It takes a person twice the work
To try to rearrange it.

There is nothing as comparable,
That's as difficult to find.
As when you finally come to realize,
That you have lost your mind.

You really haven't lost it.
The contents are still there.
It's just that you've restored them,
And you can't remember where.

I'm sure that I could hurry up
And know that I have made it.
If you would just give me a clue,
To locate where I laid it.

The Cognitive Overhaul

My speech therapist, Kathy Kaczor, was the department chairwoman. She was very knowledgeable of cognitive deficits and I think, she took a special interest in finding mine.

Many of the severe ones were in the areas of processing, memory, attention, concentration, judgment, reasoning, and general thinking skills.

I don't remember much of what Kathy and I worked on initially. But I do remember, she always seemed to find the things that were especially difficult for me.

She would urge me to try to remember things she said and did, when I was sure that she didn't say or do anything.

The days passed and the weeks passed. We sequenced. We tested. Kathy would read. I'd listen. I'd forget. She'd read it again patiently, ever patiently, over and over. Everything I needed to know had to be written in my Memory Book. She'd point to my book and tell me to use it. Then she'd have me leave it on the table and see if I could remember. I didn't. She'd remind me over and over. She'd watch me to see not only that I used it, but how and what I wrote.

Kathy wanted me to learn. I laughed with her. I cried with her. It was frustrating to know what I had lost. I was not used to being a helpless student, but that was exactly how I felt in all of my therapy sessions. Only a few months ago, I had been the teacher.

In spite of my frustrations, I began to remember to use my memory book. I wasn't ever sure it was really necessary, but Kathy wanted me to use it, so I tried to remember to use it. Bringing it with me would please Kathy and reward her efforts and insistence. So to keep her happy, I carried it with me. She never have cared why I used it, only that I did. The fact that I was using it to keep her happy accomplished the goal.

In her office there were shelves of books. My attention was continually drawn to one particular notebook on the shelf, which had darker and more dominant initials on the binding than the others. I can't tell you how often I interrupted Kathy to ask what those initials meant.

"W.A.L.C.," she told me a hundred times, I'm sure. I'd ask, she'd answer. Then she would suggest that we go on. Five minutes later, I would ask her again. I remember asking. I needed to know! There wasn't a time when I went to Kathy's office that I didn't notice that notebook. However, I don't remember to this day what the initials meant. But I did gradually learn it was inappropriate to continually ask Kathy, when we were focused on other things. I was told that showed improvement in the frontal areas of my brain. Cheers!

The clock hanging on her wall was crooked. I must have told her a thousand times. She never did straighten it. I often wonder now, if she purposely kept it crooked to distract me.

One of her primary worries was that I refused to accept a lot of my deficits as being permanent. This was especially true in areas of concentration and attention, where gains were not what she would have liked. I would tell her with all sincerity these were just temporary deficits that would go away. I was willing to do anything she wanted. I would work as hard as I could. I was sure that many of the things I couldn't do, would miraculously disappear. I knew this as a fact. It seemed she exhausted herself trying to make me accept these strategies I was learning, might be needed permanently.

I knew she was wrong, but she was so concerned with my acceptance of these deficits, that I needed to placate her. I didn't want her to worry about something that would never come to pass. I used my memory book consistently while I was there as a patient. Many of my skills did improve. I became very good at using some of the strategies, and would totally forget when and where to apply others. But Kathy persisted and so did I. She was a very patient therapist. I liked her. I just did whatever she asked.

The Physical Overhaul

My therapist in physical therapy was also concerned with my safety. She was the one who made the decision when I could begin walking on my own. There was never any question in her mind that event was a long way down the road. I wanted to show her I was only a little unsteady, and could do it myself.

Physical therapy was the only time I was allowed out of the wheelchair. I was either assigned to a therapy cot for workouts or the parallel bars for walking. I loved the bars. I'm sure it was my gymnastics training making a connection for me. But everytime I moved, I could see the worry and panic in the eyes of the therapists. They hung onto me like glue, even though I told them I was perfectly safe.

It was a long time before I realized they had a valid concern. I emptied a P.T. lab of therapists really quickly one day. Several of them on the run, caught me at 45 degrees on my way to a crash landing in the hall. I was supposed to be in my wheelchair in the therapy room.

I also loved the stairs. What joy there would be, I knew, in walking up and down stairs, or even crawling, if necessary. I just wanted to do and go. I was fitted with a leg brace that allowed me to walk steadier and safer.

Over the weeks, I progressed from the parallel bars to the hallway with assistance. I was then allowed on the hallway rail alone and finally, unassisted. But the staff was careful never to leave me unattended.

An E.M.S. machine, which electrically stimulates movement in certain muscles, helped me recognize where to exert force for the best results. I had a residual foot drop before my accident. The disruption in the brain had made it harder for me to compensate for, and counteract this problem. It hindered my recovery and made it more of a complication.

But the worst problem was my lack of judgment. The staff never knew what I would do. How could they? I didn't know myself.

One day in physical therapy, I was working on a round black disc that was elevated only in the middle. It had a round half ball in the center of the bottom, so that when you stood on it, it wobbled in all directions. I was just beginning to use it. Sarah, my physical therapist, was still a little leery of my ability to be safe. I had previously been using a roller board that was still in the area. I wondered what would happen if I put the wobbly disc on top of the rocking board and stood on top of both. Which way would I tip? I tried it.

Sarah's frantic scream scared the living daylights out of me. Panic set in and I started to cry. She sat me down, apologized for scaring me, and tried to make me understand the danger I had created for myself. I didn't understand, even then.

Together, we had serious progress to make.

BEING IMPULSIVE

..........is what you don't think of, when you think you've got it all under control.

..........is "Damn the Torpedoes. Full Speed Ahead" without the "Damning the Torpedoes."

..........is that motivation that makes you run, when you only intended to think about rising.

..........is the doing without thinking ...is the the tasting without drinking.

..........is the speed of an athlete mixed with the planning of a fool, and both happening simultaneously.

..........is the quick way to something that nobody wants you to try for fear it might work.

..........is an incitement for the mind, excitement for the soul and a rebirth for inquisition.

..........is "Four to Go" without the "One for the Money and Two for the Show". "Three to get Ready" is still in Occupational Therapy somewhere practicing.

..........is the excitement of a tie, the panic of overtime, and the intensity of sudden death all wrapped into one moment in time.

..........is the reaching for life, liberty and the instinctive pursuit of everything before it is lost.

..........is an unpremeditated act for which you can be "grey belted" for life.

..........is the taking off for the clouds, before you realize, you don't know how to land.

..........is a spontaneous X-rated play, that everyone claims they don't want to see.

..........is the chasing of the butterfly, in the beginning and in the end.

Overhaul

Occupational Overhaul

My occupational therapy (O.T.) dealt primarily with the upper extremities. I had weakness and sensory problems in my right arm and hand. After the third or fourth time I caught my hand in the spokes of my wheelchair, the therapists realized I would hurt myself without realizing. I also had developed a tendency to use the back of my wrist to help myself up to a standing position. It wasn't long after arriving that it was decided to put a brace on my right wrist and hand, to prevent further injury.

There was also concern about my lack of ability to follow through with simple tasks and to stay focused. A special grip was made for my pen. I spent days writing the alphabet over and over. We used many different devices for both sensory stimulation and strength. My hand improved and I could see the improvement.

I worked hard in O.T. because of immediate gratification. I could see my progress as the days passed. So could the therapists.

I never lost my ability to calculate and compute figures; however, my ability to follow directions was nonexistent. We worked on helping me do things in proper sequence and doing small, specific tasks with my hands. I needed to relearn many of the skills I would use in the home.

All of my therapies were designed to begin from where I was, and bring me back to where I could function again on my own. They needed my help, but I wasn't sure that I needed theirs. Nonetheless, they tried and so did I.

My brain operated only in forward mode... and at a very slow speed. The only information that seemed to stay with me, even for a little while, had to be said slowly over and over. I needed time to absorb it. They repeated and I listened. As I listened, I relearned many things.

Some things I didn't even know I needed to relearn. My therapists did.

My overhaul was underway.

TELL ME

Tell me SLOW, so I can process.
Tell me QUICK, lest I lose track.
Tell me OFTEN, so I remember.
Tell me NICE, so I come back.

Tell me CLEAR, so I can hear you.
Tell me THINGS, I need to know.
Tell me EASY, all the hardships.
Tell me HOW, I need to grow.

Tell me SOON, the things I crave for.
Tell me LATER, of the pains.
Tell me MAYBE, of tomorrows.
Tell me ALWAYS, of my gains.

Tell me SMILING, so I like you.
Tell me TRUE, so I walk straight.
Tell me PATIENT, so I listen
Tell me LOVE, so I don't hate.

Tell me VISUALLY, how to think.
Tell me WHERE, so I might be.
Tell me IF, I wander too far.
Tell me JUST, to be like me.

Tell me ALL, so I can judge it.
Tell me WHEN, the time is right.
Tell me STRAIGHT, if I can do it
Tell me IF, it's worth the fight.

Tell me LATER, of the bad times.
Tell me NOW, of all the good.
Tell me GENTLY, what is hurting.
Tell me HARD, the things you should.

Tell me ANGER, when I need it.
Tell me CARING, when I'm slow.
Tell me YOUR SIDE, when I'm guilty.
Tell me FAIR, so I can know.

Tell me STERNLY, when I falter.

Tell me HOW, to do and THEN.

Tell me SOFTLY, ever gentle.

AGAIN...AGAIN...AGAIN.

 *Fasten Seat Belts*

The *grey belt* I've mentioned, is a long canvas belt used to secure a patient in a wheelchair. Its purpose is to protect that patient who is unable to safely stand without risk of injury, from instinctively rising. The belt is secured to the wheelchair from behind, where the patient cannot undo it.

I hadn't even finished with the admission process, when I was informed by the nursing staff that I was to wear a grey belt. It was one of the hardest times I encountered in rehab. It didn't take very long; however, before the nursing staff knew they had made the right decision.

I wanted to get up so badly, I would have done anything to be able to - and I tried. I became fixated on the belt and spent hour after hour trying to get it off.

When I finally discovered how to do it, they taped it down permanently, so I couldn't get it off. It was hard for me to accept that I had to have someone with me to get up out of the wheelchair. I avoided asking for help. I wanted to be able to go to the bathroom by myself. I wanted to tell them this was not acceptable to me. But, the belt stayed on. It definitely did protect me.

The only relief I got from the grey belt, was at night when they raised the sides of my bed.

It didn't take me long to realize, that with a little bit of effort, I could work the rails down and get out. Many of my nights were spent walking precariously around my room, by leaning against the wall and hanging onto the bed. I would wait until the midnight shift came on, and my door (which faced the nurses station), would be partially closed. I even fell a couple of times; nothing was hurt but my ego.

I was considered so impulsive. It wasn't until a couple of weeks before I was finally discharged, that the staff permanently released me from the dreaded grey belt. I think even then, there were second thoughts. They had to let me up, I was scheduled to go home soon. However with each extension of my discharge date, the grey belt became a reality again.

I had always been a free spirit. I did not like to stay "within the lines." There was not a space made that could keep me in. I wanted to fly to the finish line with no one watching and end this race - with no one. I wanted to go home, at least I wanted to go at my own speed.

Fasten Seat Belts

THE GREY BELT

The hardest thing for me to deal with
Once the rehab doors were shut,
Was the feeling Donna gave me when she said,
"I'm sorry, but..."

It's for your own good, so you won't act,
before your mind decides.
If you should try to get up,
Your body will not rise.

New staff comes and old staff goes.
They shift in quick retreat.
Each of them has her own plan,
To keep me in this seat.

Here I sit in 208,
with no charge nurse in sight.
I'm going to get this grey belt off,
If it takes me half the night.

I know I'd promise anything,
If they'd let me try to walk.
I could do it by myself,
But they watch me like a hawk.

I've tried to undo all the straps,
to free myself, but then,
Along they come and shake their head
And I'm back in again.

I told them it's good therapy,
If they'd let me try alone.
They just laugh and say to wait
Til Dr. Caldwell sends me home.

How can this be a time to rest,
Like it's made out to be.
If I spend each night and day,
Just trying to get free.

Sometimes I think it's a mistake,
And I am only dreaming.
Outwardly I must escape.
Inside my head I'm screaming.

I say I'm mending excellent.
They think, just O. K.
Restoration would be easier,
If they'd take this belt away.

The stairway's blocked. The "lift" is still.
Yet, I am permanently "chaired".
I have to stay in this damned thing,
Until I've been repaired.

I think I've found the remedy...
The most effective one around.
The next time that they let me loose,
I'll tie the nurses down.

They'll plead and cry, but I won't hear.
They'll know that I have got
Their safety first and I will say,
"Gee! I'm sorry, but..."

When you grey belt a patient in,
You've clipped their wings, you know.
You've left them with no time to rest,
And with no space to grow.

Fasten Seat Belts

CHAPTER NINE

Discoveries

As I physically improved, I became a challenge to the head injury staff. Even impaired, I had enough intelligence left to think for myself, solve simple problems and create more difficult ones. The only difference was now, I was unable to solve the more difficult problems I was able to create.

I had always loved to explore new areas and had always been a traveler. My head injury accentuated that curiosity.

The second floor of the hospital became the only area where I could travel. Even with the wander-guard, I occasionally would take the elevator before anyone could stop me and suddenly, find myself in unfamiliar surroundings. It didn't seem to bother me, but it certainly did the staff. When I went to eat in the dining room on the first floor, I seemed to have a need to head for the outdoor patio. I always did prefer being outside so, naturally, out I would go. There were no alarms on the first floor. After the first couple of weeks because of safety reasons, my meals were delivered to the second floor for the rest of my stay. It helped the staff keep an eye on me and protected me from the hazards of wandering.... or so they thought.

Much to the chagrin of the medical staff, I discovered a way to by-pass the alarms. While studying my *wander guard watch* one evening with my husband and friends, I asked them how they thought it worked. Someone in the room suggested it was probably by electric eye or x-ray waves and said, "Of course, it's for your protection, Bev."

Those words seemed to trigger very distinct visualizations. My mind went immediately to my photographic film bag I used when flying. It was used for protection too. It protected my film from x-rays. This thing on my arm protected me.

"From what?" I thought.

It occurred to me that it could protect me from the alarms. If it were also covered with foil, I would be protected. The film bag covered up my film and I had to close it tight. It was lined with foil. Maybe if I wrapped foil around this watch, it would protect me too. I asked for reassurance from my visitors.

They were quick to tell me it wouldn't work.

As usual I didn't listen. My eyes scanned the room. I noticed a plant pot lined with foil on my window sill. I went over, ripped a piece of the foil off and covered the top of my wander guard. I went out to the elevators and put my arm in front of the doors. The alarms went off. I was disillusioned. The watch didn't protect anything! My first independent thinking project had failed.

During the rest of that evening, my mind would not stray from the foil and why it didn't work. It worked with my film.

Why didn't it work now?

Suddenly, I thought, "Of course!"

The foil had to go totally and tightly around the watch. While my visitors were talking among themselves, I tore off a larger piece and completed wrapping the watch.

I must have forgotten about it. It wasn't until my family and friends were leaving and we were standing by the elevators to say goodbye, that I reached up to give Gordon a kiss and noticed the foil on my arm. I was right next to the elevator doors. My arm was almost touching the alarm and nothing happened.

I was so excited and told Gordon. I had no idea he would report it for my own safety before he left the building.

By the time I returned to my room, the charge nurse was waiting for me. She said she needed to check my wander guard. I gladly showed her it was still there, already forgetting about the aluminum foil.

She said I must not use foil on the watch and wasted no time taking it off. Even though I shared with her my wonderful discovery, she smiled and still insisted I not cover the wander guard watch with foil again. Well, I was pleased with my accomplishment.

Discoveries

The danger for me was that I would cover my wander-guard with foil; forget having done so and leave the protection of the floor, unnoticed. With my cognitive deficits, the staff could not allow that to happen. But, I did not understand.

UNCHARTED FLIGHT

There are times when "going" calls
And I must be on my way.
I cannot wait for night to fall
Or go another day.

My feet begin, and I end up
Where I should fear to tread.
My legs are fine. They're not mixed up.
The trouble's in my head.

So let alarms hail my leave,
If I can just be free.
For a while there'll be a slight reprieve
For my aluminum foil and me.

God does not grant wisdom at all times to all people. I ventured forth, proud of my discovery, wanting only to go where others went before me. I had the means. I thought I knew the way.

CHAPTER   TEN

Taking Off

Now they try to tell me
NO!......for my own good.
They wish that I would stay put
Safely, like I should.

They say, I must be careful,
To stop and think and rest.
But that's against my judgment
That I use when I know best.

I know there's times, that I will try
And end up on the floor.
But these breed times that I will go
And practice all the more.

When they use the wander guard
To keep me safe instead.
I hoard all the foil I can
and "run"....full speed ahead!

The nurses patiently tried to explain to me, over and over again, that using foil to cover my wander-guard was not acceptable behavior. Yet, the freedom it brought me conflicted with this fact. This confusion was to remain a problem for the rest of my stay there.

I never realized that aluminum foil was in such abundance. During our weekly Breakfast Club, patients with head injuries were in charge of making muffins and selling them within the hospital. I found yards of aluminum foil. We used it to cover the trays and to put over the muffins. Once we had sold all the muffins, I would fold the foil and take it back to my room. At first, no one supervising the activity said anything.

The nursing staff would come in daily and confiscate the foil. Daily, I would collect more. I realized the O.T. Labs had plenty because that's where we covered the muffins, and I had that job. I tried several times to collect some from there, but the therapists always seemed to notice me collecting it and quickly volunteered to help me return it to the nurse's station.

Over the weeks, I wandered, taking my protective foil with me whenever I could get away with it. I have been told by nurses who now are friends, that they found me on other floors, in the basement, in the road, in the parking lot, in the sunshine, and in the rain. Some of the times, I remember. Many others, I don't. Perhaps it is just as well.

I recall one day while on the first floor, I decided to take an elevator back to my room, which I was not allowed to do alone. But when the doors opened onto the second floor, it suddenly dawned on me that I couldn't get out of the elevator without the alarm going off. The nurses would see me. I pushed #3 and rode up to the third floor. (There were no alarms on that floor.) As I started to wheel myself out of the elevator, I heard the voice of Mary Ellen, a regular nurse on my floor. I knew she would know I didn't belong there, so I backed into the elevator and pressed #B, the only button left. The elevator went down and the doors opened. I remember seeing a room straight ahead of me and that's all. I was found in the center of the road that day, apparently about to wheel north toward the city. I'm glad they found me.

I always hated the city.

Another night my husband had to leave the hospital early because of a meeting. He left, telling me casually, "I'll see you later." Later that evening, when he usually would have been there, I went down to the lobby to wait for him to arrive. It grew dark outside. I knew I couldn't see out and therefore, concluded that he couldn't see me. So I went outside where he could see me easier.

I was aware that it was raining hard. It didn't register that I was getting wet. I couldn't see up or down the road very well. The cars and ambulances travelled that road quite fast on their way to the Maine Medical Center Emergency Room. The entrance was directly across the street from the New England Rehabilitation Hospital. I wanted to be able to look up the street and watch for him, so I walked out into the driveway to see better.

I had on my Walkman earphones and was listening to my music. I was not the slightest bit concerned that I might not hear a car and couldn't see oncoming traffic. My only thought was helping my husband find me. I never realized I was getting drenched or worse, that I was in any danger.

Lucky for me, a nurse happened to look out the second floor lobby window and saw me.

I never really understood, at the time, why everyone was so excited. I knew I was fine and was sure I could take care of myself.

Day nurses, Donna, Sharon and Sandy, who worked with patients with head injury, persevered. They tried to reteach me that wandering was unacceptable. Every day, they would ask me for the aluminum foil in my pockets. Every day, I would give it to them.

These three were usually the ones who were responsible for me. When I used behavior that was inappropriate, they would say, quite emphatically, "We need to go to your room, Beverley, and talk...NOW, Beverley!"

I became used to these nurses' talks. We had them often. I never realized how many, until much later in my recovery.

One day, after a very long talk with Donna, she convinced me it would be better for her if I turned over all the foil I had collected... and I knew she meant ALL of it. I emptied my closet, pants, drawers and even my pillow, of hordes of the stuff.

It had become a compulsion for me to collect it, even if I never used it. As she was leaving my room, I even told her to take my plant, so she could have all my foil.

That night was the worse night of my life in rehab. Foil had become my security blanket, a necessity. It represented freedom and my knowing I could leave, if I had to.

I managed through the night, but didn't sleep much thinking about it. By morning, I had accepted that I was better off without it. When they brought my breakfast tray to me, I looked down at my food. Every dish was covered with foil!

At first, I thought the nurses were playing a trick on me. Apparently, it had been on my tray all along for weeks, but I had never noticed it. As I looked around, I suddenly realized the other patients' trays were also covered with foil. I quickly became a volunteer, helping to take the coverings off my friends' dishes and to return their trays when they were done. My foil supply was endless. I'm not sure they ever figured out why my sudden new interest in helping the other patients.

It was a wonderful surprise and a veritable smorgasbord. My night's withdrawal symptoms had been for naught and the nursing staff had to begin all over again.

My sudden desire to help other patients, would become another problem for them to deal with in the weeks ahead.

Long weeks, endless repetitions and countless strategies later, they finally succeeded in weaning me from the aluminum foil syndrome. However, first, they had to convince me not to use the stairs or elevators.

They put a large card on my tray that read:

**I MUST NOT USE THE STAIRS
OR ELEVATORS.
IT IS NOT SAFE FOR ME.**

They bordered it with neon pink, so I would see it easily. After days of reminding me to read it, the staff then had me keep the card in my right pocket. The staff was told to ask me all day what I had in my right pocket. I can remember looking over and over and finding the same card with those same words:

**I MUST NOT USE THE STAIRS
OR ELEVATORS.
IT IS NOT SAFE FOR ME.**

I don't believe I understood what the concept of "safe" meant, but the constant repetition and conscious visualization of stairs and elevators made it easier to remember.

My ability to use good judgment and make competent decisions was drastically impaired, though I didn't know it. That seems ludicrous to me now. But, I was totally unaware then. Somehow between me having impaired judgment and being terribly impulsive, the staff had a real problem.

Sometimes, I just needed to go. The nurses told me they found me one time in the parking lot, heading over to the business office to get some money. (The business office does not give out money to patients.) I had been taken to the business office once before by a therapist as part of my responsibility to pick up funds for the Breakfast Club. Somehow, my mind connected that trip with the getting money. It's odd how the mind works.

Improvement in dealing with stairs, elevators and aluminum foil did not come quickly or easily for me. It was very gradual. It was kind of like becoming aware of W.A.L.C. on Kathy Kaczor's book cover in her office. (I still was distracted, fascinated and wanted to know the meaning, but knew I shouldn't ask again.)

I never lost the distraction, the fascination and the urge to explore yet, slowly began to realize, that perhaps it was not the best thing to do at that time. I tried to wait until it was more appropriate. Sometimes, I was successful.

They told me I was slowly improving. I agreed.

 *Water Courses*

I was what you might call a *water baby*. I was raised within fifty feet of the ocean. As a child, I had spent all my free time roaming the beach and swimming in the water. I can't remember when I couldn't swim, and doubt there was ever a time I didn't.

I became a water safety instructor with the Red Cross during college, and spent my summers as a waterfront director at summer camps around Maine. I went to the first Underwater Society of America Convention held in Boston in 1959.

I was an active member of the Maine Divers' Association. I had scuba dived under ice, more than two feet thick, in the cold winds of February,

---

testing different combinations of diving suits; did icthiology studies in the spring thaw of lakes and ponds, and searched for bodies of drowning victims in the rivers in the heat of the summer. I was a veteran of the water.

It had only been three months since I was underwater off Australia on the Great Barrier Reef. I had plenty of experience when it came to swimming - and it was now August. I knew I should be swimming somewhere right now.

Much of rehabilitation therapy is finding something that was an interest to the patient. The theory is to use that interest to motivate the patient and thus, further the recovery. The hospital minister visited me one day. I told him how much I wanted to be home in my pool. He seemed surprised I wasn't in pool therapy. He said he'd look into it. I thought at the time that he was joking. God not only works in strange ways, but does it quickly. That week I was assigned to pool therapy. Not only would pool therapy be my favorite, it was also the one in which I was the most motivated and most daring.

I became weightless in the water and many movements that were difficult for me became easier. It was not that way in the beginning, however. I remember the first time I was lowered into the pool. I had to wear my leg brace (called an AFO: Ankle-Foot, Orthotic). Weights were needed on my leg to keep me to the bottom. But my weak side rose up, all I did was turn in circles. After a while, I managed to compensate. After a few more trips, I was not only staying afloat, but swimming! Initially, I could not get my right arm out of the water and had to drag it across the surface. Slowly, I managed to make my body do some of the things I wanted it to do.

The water became a source of strength for me. It gave me something to look forward to when I got depressed. I could tell I was improving by my endurance and my ability to stay down and level in the water. The therapists always had a time keeping me above water long enough to follow directions. I had found a new home where I felt comfortable and safe.

I never got as strong as I wanted, but I had a wonderful time trying. I even enjoyed exercises. I looked forward to going and, as I improved, I became more patient in my other therapies.

One day, after I had completed fourteen laps of the pool with my therapist, I was stricken with sudden pains in my chest. It felt like an elephant was sitting on me. I had a deep radiating pain in my good arm. I had no intention of telling anyone. I grabbed the side of pool and became quiet, as I tried to breathe. For me to be quiet and still was enough to make everyone know something was wrong. I managed to get out of the pool with help. But once in the locker room, I think I turned white. Though I assured Carolyn, my swim therapist, I would be fine, she wasted no time in calling an ambulance. The medics were in the locker room within two or three minutes. Within five minutes, they had an IV instituted, nitro under my tongue and I was being whisked on my way to the Maine Medical Center.

After a brief stay, tests and medication in the Emergency Room, I was eventually transferred back to New England Rehabilitation Hospital and assigned to bed.

It was only a few days though and I was back in my wheelchair. I was very grateful to be allowed up now.

But, I was never to return to swim therapy.

I think Carolyn had been more scared than I. With my memory problem, I might forget about the incident. She would remember it for a long time. She is a good friend now, and we can joke about it. But it wasn't funny, then. It was the end of my best therapy. I had always loved swimming.

CHAPTER TWELVE

Radio Check

Listening allows time to recover without being hurried; a time to escape without being chased, time to listen without being interrupted and, most of all, time to relearn without guilt. Earphones allow you to absorb, recharge or ignore whatever serves you best, in privacy.

Journeys home need songs to accompany the trip. Those songs are one of the most important pieces of luggage a survivor packs.

I loved my music. I thanked God many times during my recuperation I didn't lose that appreciation. Because of my need to escape, my cassette player and earphones were my most treasured possessions. They went with me everywhere; attached to my wheelchair and carried in my pocket when I was mobile.

I had just been to New York to see *Phantom of the Opera* a month before arriving at New England Rehabilitation Hospital. The play was still fresh in my mind. The score was the most beautiful music that I'd ever heard. It only seemed natural to keep that soundtrack close.

Those times when I needed to totally relax and get away from thinking, I would play the complete score of *Phantom of the Opera*. I would become so involved in the play that I'd forget everything else.

I had another soundtrack from a play unknown on the U.S. scene at the time, *Miss Saigon*. It had opened in London and was scheduled for Broadway in the spring. *Phantom of the Opera* and *Miss Saigon* played vital roles in my ability to deal with my rehabilitation.

I would listen *to Miss Saigon* whenever I needed to attack my problems head on, or was angry and frustrated. Though I had never seen the production, the music was one of persistence, love, determination, and courage. Listening to it, gave me strength. Those times when the hospital noise level increased and confusion reigned in the halls, I took refuge in the music.

It gave me solace. I felt others shared my feelings. I wanted to believe that none of this was really happening to me; that I would wake up and find it was all a bad dream. But for whatever reasons I listened, my music became a refuge from the reality of my situation.

At night when things were still, I was often awake. There were no therapies, no time limits, no commitments. I lived in my music, without worry that I might miss someone's verbal directions. I relaxed. I became whatever I wanted and went wherever the music carried me. In the darkness, like the phantom, I would start a journey and the music would set me free.

My music became my haven from the real world. It kept me from feeling alone. I don't mean physically alone. Music made me feel whole again. In my music no one ever said anything too fast for me to comprehend. I never needed to ask for repetition. If I became distracted, no one had to tell or remind me; and if I didn't remember what I just heard, no one cared.

I would let myself cry with the music. I couldn't allow myself to cry for me. The important thing was that I allowed my tears to fall, and because I thought they were falling for someone else, it was OK. I needed to be very careful to only play other songs I knew by heart. My brain was not able to deal with "new" words.

No one else could ever intrude into my private world of song, unless I chose to let them in; that put me back in control.

Actually, the music and I needed each other. After all, without me, there was no one to hear the music. It was so special, it demanded listening.

I used the music to soothe the hurt and to fight the anger. It somehow put some meaning into the senseless world in which I found myself. Never did I put on my earphones and turn on the volume, that there wasn't always someone there waiting to sing for me.

We had a lot in common, Miss Saigon, the Phantom and I. The three of us were locked in worlds we couldn't escape from, had memories of other times and places, we were all trying desperately to find a way out. Whether it was from the darkness, the squalor or the loneliness of the night really made no difference in the end.

I developed a special closeness to music, and the soundtracks from those plays, in particular, during my rehabilitation...a fondness that would continue to grow for a very long time.

Won't you please sing for me
a melancholy song?
And transport me to where I'm
safe, back where I belong.

CHAPTER THIRTEEN

Proper Procedure

There was a patient on my floor named Tim.

He was also a head injured patient. Tim would often try to grab the nurses, hug and kiss them, thinking they were his daughter.

He would say his daughter's name and then, reach for the nurse. Tim was in the "grab mode" this particular night, and had continually tried to kiss the passing nurses.

There was a nurse who worked on the unit that evening who had a tremendous Irish brogue. I never saw her again, but I'll never forget her.

When the med carts were completed, she sat down with Tim. Everytime he would reach for her face, she would say, "No, Tim. Families kiss. Friends shake hands."

Then, she would take his hands and hold them. A few seconds later, he would struggle to kiss her. She would grab his hands and say, "No, Tim. Families kiss. Friends shake hands. We are friends, Tim. Friends shake hands. What do friends do, Tim? Friends shake hands."

This went on all evening.

I could not believe this nurse's patience and effort. She must have repeated the same words close to a hundred or so times that night. Each time in the same patient tone, and with the same obvious caring and love.

However, after a couple of hours, my brain started to repeat, "Families kiss and friends shake hands."

I had to wheel myself into my room and put on my earphones to drown out the never-ending scene. Even in the middle of the love songs, I could hear in the background, "Families kiss, friends shake hands."

I knew exactly what was happening in the hall. On and on throughout the evening, I heard the words and Tim's muttering in response to her. I even thought I sensed a change in him over the course of the night, but it was probably both a desired and imagined response on my part.

When I later returned to the hall, they were still there and I wondered...what if his friends were like mine. We kiss; a warm, social acknowledgment on the cheek. I even wondered if that was an inappropriate thing to do, but decided it would be better if I didn't ask or interfere. I hid again within my earphones. I cranked up the volume and watched in pure amazement at the moving lips and grabbing hands, both in tune with each other and with my music.

I learned something that night and it never disappeared from my memory. I think part of it was the value of repetition. It also was the wonder of patience and the art of caring.

Someone I had never seen before and was destined to never see again, had gotten through to me. I had learned proper procedure, that families kiss and friends shake hands...even though Tim never quite figured it out.

CHAPTER FOURTEEN

Cockpit Changes

Slowly as I improved, the realization of danger made its presence known in my brain as something to be avoided. Those sounds of the alarms that before meant nothing to me, suddenly began to breed a silent, deep, inner fear each time they went off. Now I was beginning to realize that they meant danger ... and I needed to get away from them.

In a hospital, those sounds are always there. They go off all day and night. Many patients set them off. I had no control of when they went off, yet each time they did, I thought that I had done it. I felt an urgent need to take control, shut them off and get myself out of danger.

I think it was that fear that later, became the basis for my need to escape from situations in which I felt afraid.

Looking for Changes

Over the ensuing weeks, I became depressed. I wanted out! I was unable to see an end to my rehabilitation. Although it was obvious I was making progress, it was not fast enough for me. I wanted things to change overnight, so I could see the results. My therapists stayed with me and kept me working and busy every minute. I did not have time to get distracted and my rehabilitation continued without interruptions.

Even though I was slowly realizing I had become a different person, the impact of that fact was more important. I was beginning to not like myself anymore. I wanted to tell everyone that this person they were dealing with as a patient wasn't the *real me*.

They didn't even know the real ME.

This person they were dealing with on a day-to-day basis was slow, forgetful, absent-minded, unable to pay attention to anything, incapable of success, and usually seemed to do what wasn't appropriate.

She lacked judgment and just plain common sense. I wanted OUT. I needed to get away from this person whom I no longer knew or liked.

It was my foil that gave me an escape. How could these therapists continue working with me? Didn't they know it wasn't the real me they were treating. I knew that I could do anything. They needed to know that too.

> This is not ME
> Within this chair.
> Someone else
> Is sitting there.
>
> Where I've gone
> I do not know.
> But I need help
> Before you go.
>
> Helping "her"
> Will help me do
> All the things
> You want me to.
>
> But what you get
> Is what you see.
> Just be aware
> This is not ME.

Much more importantly to me, I was and always had been a leader. I never had to depend on others. I faced any and all adversities, and solved them with fairness, consistency and diplomacy. I had been well known among my colleagues as being the ultimate in calmness and confidence. They would never be able to understand what had happened to me. I couldn't understand what had happened to me. Therefore, I reached an acceptable conclusion. This was not ME.

There's an old saying:

"When you are up to your ass in alligators, it is difficult to remember that your initial objective was to drain the swamp."

The confidence I always had in the past was disappearing. I now found that my emotional gears were stuck. I was fighting to regain control; the alligators were all around and my initial objective was somewhere having therapy. I couldn't remember where or why!

EMOTIONAL COMMUNICATION

Sometimes it isn't always clear,
What I mean to say.
I try to make you understand,
In a different sort of way.

Some things I don't know how to put,
Or what I'm all about.
I want to know what angers me
But something else comes out.

I really want to join the game.
But no longer dare to play it.
I really want to share myself.
But don't know how to say it.

I know that I can face the truth,
And not fear, if I'm rejected.
And yet, when the truth comes out,
Its not what I expected.

When I improve and I can speak
Without that dreaded fear,
That all my words will tumble out,
Before my brain's in gear...

Til then, it's hard to share the words
Of how I'm really feeling.
Maybe it will change with time,
When I am finished "healing".

This non-acceptance of myself probably served to push my motivation to *full steam ahead*. I never missed a therapy session. In fact, I begged and pleaded for more. I don't think the hospital ever had such a motivated and determined patient. As I persevered, improvements became more noticeable to me and the hospital staff. However, no matter how much progress I made, the *wanderguard* remained locked onto my wrist. I was watched 24 hours a day, because I would forget and wander.

In late September after six weeks of therapy, I was finally released from the wheelchair and allowed to walk with a brace. It was like an early Christmas present. I felt I had worked harder to get this present than anything I had ever earned before. Being free of my wheelchair opened new doors. I was now able to get away and do things. I could feel needed again. I practiced walking up and down the corridors, sometimes halfway into the night. I was making great strides with my physical therapy. I knew the therapists were thrilled with my progress.

In speech therapy, I was still having trouble paying attention and was easily distracted, though some areas showed much improvement. We continued to work hard developing new strategies for those areas that didn't.

I spent many late evenings alone watching gymnastic meets on video in the conference room. I not only practiced scoring the routine, but when I finished a routine, I would replay it over and over and correct what I had missed. I spent countless hours practicing my shorthand; writing smaller and smaller each time, to cram as much information as I could in the area allowed on the scoresheet. I remembered the judging shorthand symbols. Doctors said it was overlearned information. I only had to learn to write them legibly. That was a big task. It was the most important one for me because I planned to get back to judging just as soon as they let me out of the hospital. Even I knew, there were adjustments to make to do that.

Kathy, my speech therapist, would go over my notes with me each day. We would find mistakes and correct them together. We would review problems I had encountered with my video judging from the night before, and devise strategies to compensate. The next night I would be back to work. As part of my therapy, I would give speeches to Kathy about the sport of gymnastics. She became knowledgeable, as I improved. She would also have me listen to her give speeches about topics strange for me. We would see if I could listen and retain.

I also had a problem with the alphabet. I knew it. My ability to put anything in alphabetical order was almost nil. It would take me forever, and only then, if someone didn't interrupt me. We would just seem to conquer one deficit and Kathy would find another. When I finally could remember four numbers in a row, she worked on five. When I became better at solving two sentence problems, she did three sentence ones. She put forth so much time and effort devising ways for me to relearn. I recorded them all very diligently in my memory book. She checked my book twice every day to see that I did.

I became more knowledgeable of things I could and couldn't do. My ability to take control of myself and my knowing where I was at all times, became of prime importance. Being free of my wheel chair helped me set new sights and new horizons in my determination, and worked to rebuild my confidence.

CHAPTER FIFTEEN

Charity Flight

A week or so later, I had a chance to prove my determination and ability to take care of myself and others, and help someone else in the process.

One evening, the phone rang at the nurses' station outside my door. It was Dottie calling. She was a CNA from the night shift and had been particularly friendly to me during her late evening shifts. When I would have the urge to wander, she would take me with her downstairs on her break.

Paula, the charge nurse, answered the phone and said that Dottie was in Maine Medical Center (across the street) in Room 723 as a patient. Dottie just wanted to say, "Hi" to everyone.

A patient's call light came on. Paula had to leave the nurse's station to answer it. I heard her ask Dottie if she'd like to talk to me for a minute until she returned.

Taking the telephone, I asked Dottie how she was feeling. She said actually, she was quite hungry. They hadn't let her eat anything all day because of tests. I told her I only had an orange and an apple left, but she was more than welcome to have them, if she wanted. I even offered to bring them over personally.

It didn't take her long to respond with a very definite, "Absolutely not, Bev. I'll be fine. Don't even THINK about it."

I could read between the lines though. I knew she was really hungry and probably very lonesome. I decided that I would go and visit her. It was the least I could do for her.

When Paula came back and took the phone, I went into my room, put on my shoes, wrapped aluminum foil around my wander guard, stuffed my apple and orange in my pocket, and headed for the back stairs.

I opened the door to the outer steps at the side of the building. A CNA was sitting there taking a break. She looked up, saw me, and said in surprise, "Beverley! What are you doing out here?"

I told her that Dottie needed help. She was hungry and I was taking her some food. She looked confused. I knew she didn't understand. I certainly didn't have the time to explain it to her.

She, however, wasted no time in assuring me that my trip was impossible. I wasted no time in assuring her that the trip was a fact. She could either pretend she hadn't seen me or come along as a spectator, if she thought I needed protection. But I WAS going. She knew that there was no physical way for her to stop me. She decided to go with me, try to talk me out of my venture and walk me back. She was very unsuccessful.

She kept complaining that all the doors at the Maine Medical Center would be locked. (It was now 9:30 p.m.) I told her she should be more positive, Dottie needed this food.

When we arrived at the front door, there was a sign that read "Have Your Passes Ready."

I knew I didn't have a pass. The CNA said she would get fired if she got caught. I remember reminding her, that if she had a pass, we wouldn't have a problem. Besides we were doing something good, not bad. I asked her to calm down because I needed to think.

I grabbed her by the arm and we started for the side door. It was locked. She wanted to go back, but I was sure that where there was a will, there was a way. Dottie was waiting for this food.

I was familiar with the emergency entrance because of my trip there by ambulance from swimming therapy, and I spent each night watching the ambulances pull in and out of the parking lot. The next logical step was to try those doors. I knew they would be open at this time of night. Besides this was an emergency!

I literally dragged the CNA to the doors; we entered unnoticed, with all the other commotion going on. She was really a nuisance to my efforts. If I could deal with this distraction, I could deal with anything. She kept insisting that we'd get caught. I tried to comfort her and told her if we got in trouble, I would scream. She could then say I had left without permission, and she was chasing me. She seemed to quiet down a bit after that. Maybe she went into shock; at least she kept quiet.

Despite her reluctance, I found the way to the elevators. She said we didn't even know what room Dottie was in. I really surprised her when, from out of my right pocket, I pulled a piece of paper with #723 written on it.

I had been programmed by experts. She should have known that.

We got on the elevator and when the doors opened on the 7th floor, we saw the nurses station. The CNA was a nervous wreck. I took her hand and assured her everything would be OK. I began to wonder why I had even offered to bring her.

Knowing the CNA would follow, I found room 723 all by myself. Kathy, my speech therapist, would be very proud of me, if she could see the confidence with which I handled this situation.

As we entered the room, Dottie looked up and said, "I knew it. Somehow I knew you'd be here. Bev."

I answered, "Of course!"

Proud I hadn't disappointed her, I took the apple and orange out my pocket and gave them to my friend. It felt good to be able to give back some of the care, attention and time she had given me.

I couldn't stay long. Everyone seemed so nervous, except me. But I didn't mind leaving now. I knew Dottie wasn't going to be hungry, and besides, I had to get this CNA back before she got caught and we got in trouble.

We left as openly and discreetly as we had come. When we got across the street, I left the CNA on the steps outside to recover.

I went directly to my room, took off my shoes, returned to my wheelchair, (I only used it now to sit in) and resumed my place in front of the nurses' station...very pleased.

Not long after, Paula returned. She looked over at me and said "Gee, Bev, I'm pleasantly surprised. I really thought you'd try to go to see Dottie."

I told her she didn't have to worry. I already had. Paula looked at me with the "what are you saying" expression. I think she knew I was not confabulating. I hadn't planned to tell her of my trip, but when she brought up the subject, the words just came out. I was proud of how I had just handled a very difficult situation. I reiterated to Paula that she didn't have to worry. I even suggested she call Dottie; I could see she was still unsure. I didn't want her to worry all night that I might leave.

She knew now she had to pick up the phone and find out for herself. But, I also knew she really didn't want to know. She doubted that I could have done it so quickly, especially without her knowing. Dottie confirmed her growing suspicion.

When she hung up the phone, I told her, "It was really OK. Although I knew I could get to Dottie's room myself, I had not gone alone. I had kidnapped a CNA to protect me.

She said, "WHO?"

I told her I couldn't tell her that or she might get fired. (Obviously, she would know shortly when the CNA returned from break.)

Paula said nothing. There was no need to. She just shook her head. I knew she understood ... and she was pleased with my progress.

I had finally begun to ask for help.

Before one can fly, one needs to conquer the mountain of obstacles that impede the search for wings.

CONQUERING THE HEIGHTS

Dear God, give me mountains
with hills at their knees,
Ones much too tall
for the flutter of trees.

Mountains that know
the pale shadow of death,
That have kissed a bright star
and felt its first breath.

Bring on the biggest
and tallest you store,
Ones that have never
been conquered before.

Ones where the peaks,
touch the top of the sky,
And part only for clouds
as they slowly pass by.

Mountains that cherish
life's golden rimmed cup.
Yes, God! Give me mountains
and the strength to climb up.

CHAPTER SIXTEEN

OnThe Runway

As I approached the time scheduled for my discharge as an inpatient, I was making rapid strides in improvement. I felt great. However, my therapists still held their own view on things.

Meeting with Gordon and me, my occupational therapist explained what we could expect in the future. My attention and processing would continue as problems, and I would need supervision at all times. I thought, "God! This can't be me, she's describing. I've come such a long way!"

My physical therapist insisted that I was not aware of my physical limitations, got easily distracted and was not safe to be left alone. Each time I tried something, it was still without thinking.

I was still extremely impulsive. Although I knew she was sincerely interested in my welfare, she was just not aware of how much I could do completely by myself. And I had made great strides in walking unassisted.

My speech therapist said I still had serious attention deficits and was in a state of denial. My own safety was in jeopardy, I needed to learn to concentrate and pay more attention.

My team insisted a memory book was vital to my rehabilitation. I would have to continue to use it, or I would not be able to function alone. I thought, surely once I left the hospital, all the formalities of therapy would be left behind too - like this memory book of mine. I couldn't imagine I'd have to use it forever!

I wrote in it when someone reminded me. I tried to remember. Sometimes, just seeing it would be a reminder in itself. The staff made sure I carried it everywhere. Their constant reminders to write things down was building a repetitive format with which I, unknowingly, was being taught to compensate and survive.

I accepted the therapists' views as sincerely theirs and well intended, but was still unable to believe them as being true, much less descriptive of me and my future.

Although my husband had visited me in the hospital every day I was there, and I loved him dearly, I was afraid to go home. I was afraid to even think about being on my own. I knew I wandered and didn't know if I would be safe. I felt protected and secure in the hospital. I'd come to trust the staff, even though I did not totally believe everything they said about me yet.

Being on the runway, preparing to take off, can be very frightening.

A Try On My Own

Earlier in my stay at the hospital, I had been a given an overnight pass to go home. The therapeutic overnight is meant to give the patient an opportunity to test their home environment. Upon return to the hospital, therapists can then work to correct those problem areas the patient encountered. My overnight probably came earlier than it should have. I was unaware of the purpose of the overnight, but was very glad to get out of the hospital.

Once home, it wasn't long before I wished I was back within the safety of the hospital. The problem that affected me the most at home was one I didn't understand at the time, and so, had never discussed.

The only room of my home that I felt safe in was the upstairs bedroom. At first, I attributed this to sexual reasons and didn't think too much about it. When I was downstairs in the living areas, I felt like I didn't belong there; that I was in some strange place that wasn't mine.

I would later come to realize that only about one week before I went into the hospital, we had completely redecorated the first floor of our home. We had put in new carpets and linoleum, appliances, furniture, and repainted walls. Therapists would determine months later, that my brain had not stored this new information and indeed, I was really in somebody else's house.

I found it very distracting, tiring and a constant source of uneasiness. I couldn't wait to get back to the hospital. I tried not to let Gordon see my uneasiness, but I'm sure he was aware of it. Judgment and safety were real problems. I seemed to have no idea of the seriousness of either.

Aside from everything else, I had a fear of leaving the hospital. Perhaps if I had been working on coping skills, this fear would have been detected.

Later I learned, this is a normal fear, arising from any long confinement, but especially for people with head injury. No one told me then it was OK to feel afraid. I wasn't afraid of much, but leaving the safety of the hospital petrified me. I'm sure other head-injury patients have felt the same fear, but can't or haven't expressed it.

I should have anticipated this fear or, at least, figured out why I was afraid. Any change I had to deal with became a source of conflict. From the very beginning of my hospitalization, I remember my fear that Dr. Story would not remain in charge. There were other examples. My therapists would be rotated so all had a chance to deal with different kinds of patients...the amputees, oncology, head injured. I dreaded changing therapists. Every time one changed, I lost a part of myself. I thank God I had as few changes as I did. The most successful element of therapy for patients with head injury is consistency.

My discharge date was postponed as the therapists, pleased at my continued progress, requested extensions. I, too, recognized that I was improving.

In early October, I was discharged because my insurance company refused to continue my coverage as an in-patient. The doctors worked out an agreement whereby the insurance company agreed to cover 100% of out-patient costs for me instead of the more expensive in-patient expenses. Gordon and I were informed of this decision only a couple of days before the discharge date, so plans came fast.

The second floor staff had a formal cutting of my wander-guard, but not until they had formally placed my in-patient discharge papers in my husband's hand.

There were last minute tears as I hugged the people who had become my extended family. I am sure, as I went into the elevator, there was a sigh of relief from each staff member. They no longer had to worry about where I was going.

One of my biggest disappointments during my hospitalization, was that I had to return plane tickets meant to carry me to New Orleans for the National Gymnastics Conference. I had been very disappointed. Since I was scheduled to still be in the hospital, doctors told me I would also miss the Regional Conference as well. However, I was determined to be there. I had been at the Conference 14 consecutive years and didn't want to break my record. As it turned out, it was scheduled to start the day I was being discharged. Dr. Caldwell, my physiatrist, had earlier insisted I shouldn't go. I had been so depressed. Now suddenly, there was a chance I would make it. Gordon said if it meant that much to me, he would go with me and drive me directly there from the hospital. The Conference was being held in Rye, New York. (What we do for love!. Gordon never liked gymnastics.) I was going to make it there after all. I was ecstatic!

The hospital staff gave me plenty of suggestions about what not to do, and do, and be wary of.

I was nervous about setting out on my own. It was a strange feeling for me. The nursing staff could not believe I was heading straight for New York from the hospital, but they also knew it was useless to tell me I shouldn't.

I knew I would be fine.

I lasted one day at the conference. Between the noise, the confusion and being totally exhausted, I told my husband I was ready to head home early. The staff had been right, but I was never going to admit it. It had been MY decision.

Soon after my return, our son arrived from England and my dear friend, Pat Zeitlin, from Rhode Island came to visit. It was busy, but Pat was a refreshing, daily companion.

On the following Monday morning I arrived at the hospital with a 75 pound fruit basket for the second floor staff. Pat and I had wrapped each piece of fruit in aluminum foil. They enjoyed the fruit. They laughed at the wrapping. I know they appreciated the remembering.

It was an indication from me that I was now free and able to continue my trek in search of wings because of their knowledge, patience, understanding, and that very special caring. I think they knew that, too.

CHAPTER SEVENTEEN

Ground School

I continued at New England Rehabilitation Hospital as an outpatient with physical therapy, occupational therapy and speech therapy each, three times a week.

The hospital insisted that I have supervision, at all times, at home. My husband or one of my daughters was always with me. A C.N.A. was hired from a home health agency to stay with me five hours a day. She supervised my daily care, gave my husband a break, helped me with areas that needed work, and made sure that I didn't burn the house down.

On my own, I had to take stock of myself and start to build on what I had left. I became aware of other problem areas I hadn't encountered in the hospital setting.

Instead of being my former social bug self, I was now uncomfortable and hesitant. My confidence in my ability to function disappeared and I, unconsciously, took on the role of passive observer.

I found myself avoiding crowds, meetings, any function that required me to take part, or to make conversation. When I met my old colleagues, I was unable to initiate or carry on a meaningful conversation.

I developed panic attacks. In strange situations where I had no control, I ran. If I was over-stimulated and couldn't quiet myself, I ran. If I sensed danger, (the presence of too many people, or being closed in a room with the exit blocked) I ran.

When at the hospital for out-patient therapy, if I heard the wander-guard alarms going off or the sounds of a person in pain, the need to escape would be overwhelming.

My therapists said that I always had this fear, but never realized it. Well, I was starting to realize it now, and had to find a solution fast. These problems were affecting my recovery.

I was assigned extra therapy sessions at the hospital, including relaxation and handling of stress. These were prior sources of strengths of mine and it was very clear that suddenly, they were my weaknesses. Understanding and coping in these areas became a necessity.

Gordon never knew what to expect. He always worried about my "taking off" by myself. I guess he probably had reason to. My wander guard was gone and I went quieter now.

One instance he reminds me of, even now, was when he told me the local Sunday newspaper would no longer be delivered to our house. He told me about it on a Saturday night. The following morning, I awoke at 5:30 a.m. and came downstairs. Gordon usually got up before me, but he didn't on this particular morning - or so I thought.

I saw there was no paper for him, so I decided to walk down to the local convenience store and buy one. I would be back before he awoke and I thought, he would be pleased.

I left him a note that said I had gone for a walk. I didn't want him to know where. It would be a surprise!

I put a jacket over my pajamas and I walked over a mile to the store, only to find it closed. (It opens at 8 a.m. and it was only 6 a.m.) At the same time I saw it was closed, I also realized I had forgotten to bring any money to pay for the paper. I decided to walk uptown to my daughter's house and borrow some money from her to buy the paper.

I could not go back without completing what I had set out to do. My thinking was very organized. I was pleased with myself that I didn't panic.

Well, needless to say, before I had gone much further, our truck appeared over the horizon. Gordon was driving and he looked very glad to see me. I was disappointed when I saw him. Now, I couldn't surprise him with the Sunday paper.

It took a very long discussion and explanation of the incident before I had any inkling that, perhaps, there had been danger in what I did. Perhaps, I had not thought it out enough. Just maybe, I hadn't made a good decision.

I'm not sure that my husband ever slept as sound again in the months ahead.

He continued to watch me closely. One day, he about scared me to death when he let out a bloodcurdling scream. I had my hand down in the garbage disposal and was about to switch it on, without thinking. Although he saved my hand, my ego died a coward's death. I cried for hours.

There were other deficits that came to light. I had trouble remembering how to operate my microwave. I tended to forget to shut off stove burners and the oven. You might say I encountered the "out of sight, out of mind" syndrome. If something was not in my line of vision, it would be forgotten.

One time, I was making some toast in our four-slice toaster. I put two slices in the front part and noticed I had put a folded dish towel over the back two slots. I remarked to myself that wasn't a good place to leave my towel. I never thought to move it off the toaster. So, not connecting the two facts, I pushed down the lever and started making my toast. I only realized something was wrong when I smelled the burning dish towel.

Luckily, I was able to grab it and throw the flaming towel into the sink. I was proud of my fast thinking and reactions. I was getting good.

I would start a task, get distracted by phone calls and leave the task half-done. Several times while using a cutting knife, I would be distracted, but continue to carry the knife around with me. Then I'd wonder, "Why on earth am I holding a knife?"

I needed visual reminders and cues on my walls to help me remember.

When going out into the community, I had trouble remembering to look for cars when I crossed the street and always forgot to check the traffic lights.

The C.N.A. was friendly and outgoing. We worked hard on deciphering the specific help I needed or wanted. Sometimes the two were all together different.

By Christmas, I was doing very well. I was functioning and surviving. Maybe others didn't trust me yet, but I trusted myself.... not outside in traffic, but in my home. I could even laugh at some of the problems.

In Search of Wings

Ground School did have
some humorous moments.

I CAN'T REMEMBER MORNING

I can't recall this morning. It went I don't know where.
When I went to find it. It wasn't even there.
There must have been a morning. I think it came and went.
I can't remember morning, but my energy's all spent.
I think perhaps, the sun was out...for sure I cannot say.
I might have done a lot of things, before it went away.
I thought I did my laundry and hung my clothes out fine.
But when I went to take them in, they were not on the line.
I obviously changed the linens on the master bedroom bed.
Cause now the head is at the foot, the foot is at the head.
I must have gotten groceries too, because recently I found.
The milk inside the linen closet and bags upon the ground.
I now must do things differently, than I did yesterday.
Because I won't remember, when the morning slips away.
I think I'm growing old and at the same time, growing dumb.
But then, I stop and ponder. Did morning really come?
I can't remember what I did, or who I met or when.
Somehow I hope this morning, doesn't slip away again.
For with it goes the memories of all the time I've spent
looking for the mornings that have come so fast and went.
I think of all the unknown things, that now my mind has hid.
I might even cure myself, if I could remember what I did.
I know I'm not the only one, whose mornings can't be found.
If I don't stop, and take a moment, just to write them down.
I wish I could retrieve the time, that fate has blown away.
But I can't remember mornings, if they decide to slip away.
I hope this problem changes and it changes really soon.
For possibly tomorrow, I'll be forgetting afternoon.

In Search of Wings

CHAPTER EIGHTEEN

Pilot's Log

The best truth I was ever told and the most beneficial information I received at the hospital, was the necessity of a memory book.

To some, it can be best described as part calendar, part diary, part reminders, and part vital information.   In short, it becomes an addendum to your brain. I had always used a date book to keep track of my busy schedule, but to know that now I could not even survive without a memory book, was devastating.

I realized how helpless I was without it. Without it, I had no idea where I was headed and no record of where I'd been.

There had been great truth in my speech therapist's words, "You will need to keep your book with you at all times and use it."

I suddenly found that I was completely dependent on what I relegated to the pages of my book. My past became what I wrote. Things that did not get recorded, got forgotten. I have now recovered to the point where I do not question my book. I utilize it. I carry it with me everywhere. It tells me what I did, what I have to do, who I have seen, a record of all my phone calls, important events, and a separate vital section called "long term information." This is information about cues and reminders I constantly need to remember, in order to survive each day because of my deficits. I never dreamed that what Kathy had been constantly telling me would ever come to pass. I had thought the book was just for the hospital; a part of therapy, not to be the key to my future.

During all my out-patient therapy sessions, we discussed the contents I had stored in my book. We talked. I learned. They reinforced. I repeated. There was a feeling of mutual concern for my welfare. We went over my memory book page by page and all the problems I'd worked through. We discussed those I still had to work on and those that needed extra help .

I needed to face the reality that my recovery was a continuing process. Even though I had a problem admitting it, I wasn't excellent yet.

HEARINGS IN THE HALL

"Hi Bev, How are you doing?"   "EXCELLENT"
We need to go to your room and talk!
Right.   Right.   Right.
Jones......109......confidential......
What time will the sun come out today? It will.
"Hi Bev, How are you doing?"   "EXCELLENT"
and there she is.....#66
CLUNK, the bathroom's taken. Try again later..
Oh No! She's gone again!
What's for lunch today?
"Hi Bev, How are you doing?"   "EXCELLENT"
Excuse me.....Behind you.....Could you hold the door?
Hi there, Where are you headed? Can I help?
Its part of the Disney way.....anything you want?
"Hi Bev, How are you doing?"   "EXCELLENT"
Use the stairs if you are able.
Oh God! Who set it off this time?
Squeeze my hand as hard as you can.
Hey Lady, Can you undo this belt, so I can get up?
"Hi Bev, How are you doing?"   "EXCELLENT"

A Space To Fly

CHAPTER NINETEEN

Introduction to Soloing

By January, I managed to convince the medical staff that it was not a help, but a hindrance, to be supervised. I needed the opportunity to be left on my own on a limited basis. I felt I was ready.

The CNA in my home was replaced that same day with an Occupational Therapist who was more qualified to deal with my distinctive needs, and could address my deficits more thoroughly and more intricately.

The therapist started community mobility training and worked with me in the kitchen. She worked less hours with me than the CNA had, but now it was therapy, instead of just supervision.

I was allowed to be left alone for certain defined periods of time. I actually began to look forward to my time alone each day and planned for it. I worked on my computer, with my earphones on, so I did not get distracted by the phone or other household noises. As long as I was listening to music, I would tend to continue with my task until it was completed.

I was able to answer the phone and write down messages for Gordon with more certainty now. With supervision, I was able to go shopping for a specified list of items. I was certain I could take care of myself.

My family saw definite improvements. My therapists were seeing them too. A continuing problem, obvious to all, was that I found it hard to set limits. At home one morning, I had planned to make "Texas" muffins. I only intended to make six or eight. By the time Gordon got home, I had made 48 and would have continued, if I had not been interrupted. We had a freezer full of muffins for a very long time. We decided to keep less baking ingredients on hand, to curb the chance that the same thing would happen again.

I found it hard to set limits for myself. If there was a gymnastics meet in the state, I was there. If there was seminar or meeting scheduled, I was there. Dr. Caldwell urged me to slow down. The vocational rehab counselor urged me to go slower. My family wanted me to take things a little slower, but that had always been a hard thing for me to do.

Now, it had become a real problem.

On two occasions, my husband took me to the emergency room at Stephens Memorial Hospital for pains that seemed to be in my chest and upper back. After the second visit, the emergency room doctor diagnosed an inflamed gall bladder. I could have been admitted that evening with the surgeon on call, or see my own surgeon in the morning. He gave me some demerol and for the night, I felt better. I knew I would be able to have Dr. Story. I knew I could still trust him.

The next morning Gordon and I met with Dr. Story. My ultrasound tests showed that I had gallstones and scar tissue. We decided to have the gall bladder removed.

He told us about a new procedure called laparoscopic cholecystectomy, which usually involved only an overnight hospital stay. Recovery was safer and easier than regular surgery. He strongly recommended using it. Dr. Story offered to refer us to other physicians who had performed this operation, since he had not done this one on his own yet. He also told us that the local hospital, Stephens Memorial, had to rent the equipment for this operation. Dr. Story did not in any way encourage us to use him as the surgeon, but said he would be willing to perform the operation, if we made that choice. He encouraged us to contact other physicians.

We sought the advice of a friend who was a surgeon in a nearby city and who had done hundreds of these surgeries. He suggested we ask each physician we contacted how many of these procedures he or she had performed. If it was less than ten, he advised we seek a more experienced surgeon. He would be willing to do it, if I wanted.

I was under a lot of pressure from family and friends to use him. But it would have meant that I would be in another town and in an unknown hospital. I had reservations about that.

I had fears as to how I would react to a strange place, with my tendency to wander and my inability to deal with change.

Surgery was scheduled two weeks later. Dr. Story would do it. No one totally agreed with my decision, but I had made up my mind. Dr. Story had done numerous conventional gall bladder surgeries and assured us if he ran into any problems, he would do that procedure. I'm sure he was more nervous about doing it, than I was about having him do it.

I had learned to appreciate and admire anyone attempting to "solo." I knew first hand there was something special and exciting about first attempts, being solely responsible. You give it your best shot and put that extra bit of care into it. I also knew through past experience that I could totally trust Dr. Story.

I went in for surgery on a Tuesday at 8 a.m. and was eating my favorite salad, delivered by my daughter from a local restaurant, at 3 p.m. that afternoon. Though eating solid food was not approved yet, it tasted so good.

I was home and back to my therapy sessions two days later. I felt pleased, knowing I had made a good decision on my own. I felt great physically. Now I could get back on track with other more important things in life.

I went back to judging, though still considered too much by my therapists. I had to be picked up and delivered back to my home. Gordon would get up at 5 a.m. on some days to connect me with my ride, and then often have to make an hour's ride at 11:30 p.m. to pick me up. Judging was not as easy as it once had been. But, I knew I had to do it.

I still got very frustrated, if I had to make a spontaneous decision. I found it very hard to keep my mouth shut, until I had decided exactly what it was I wanted to say; fearful that what might come out would make no sense, or be inappropriate. I disliked the strategies I now had to use and the slowness with which I functioned. But without them, I knew I would be unable to continue judging. When each routine and performance ended, I would look down at my exact shorthand in that tiny work space. I knew and remembered just how much I had improved and how far I had come, since those nights in the conference room with the VCR.

The fact that I could go and do some of the things I loved to do again, made it worth it, even if other people still had to be with me. It was the first step toward independence.

 *Navigating*

My gall bladder surgery happened on my birthday in February. Gordon decided to give me a gift of four orchestra seat tickets to a preview showing of *Miss Saigon* in New York on April 3. He told me I could invite any couple I wanted to go with us. The tickets were his way of acknowledging how much this music had meant to me. What could be more appropriate than seeing one of the shows whose soundtrack had carried me through.

I wanted to share it with people who had helped me along the way. I wanted to invite Donna and Tony Levesque from the hospital. They both had done so much in giving me support and help when I needed it most , I wanted to be able to give them something back. He agreed.

I was a little hesitant to ask Donna. I didn't know if it was something that would interest her. She assured me that she would love to go. I went to the lab to ask Tony. He assured me that he would love to go. So it was set. They were looking forward to the trip. We made plans, not only to see the show, but to see some of the city as well. We would be adventurers.

We planned an overnight trip and looked forward to it with much anticipation and excitement. Since Gordon and I only had a sports car and a truck (neither large enough to carry four people), we decided to rent a Lincoln Town Car and make the long ride in first class comfort.

Gordon decided I should become the navigator and read the maps. Planning the trip became part of my therapy sessions. My therapists and I worked practicing what would soon be a real-life situation for me. I wrote down lists of things to do, be careful of, and to remember.

Together, my support team had made many advance arrangements to see that I knew how to navigate and use my strategies to build confidence.

We picked up Donna and Tony at their home the night before the show. Gordon drove all the way and I deciphered the map and routes. I made some mistakes by getting east and west mixed up several times, but it made the trip more exciting.

By the time we finally crossed over the bridge into Lower Manhatten, we had all seen the New York City skyline many times and from many different directions. We laughed together. Good thing, we were not in a hurry. Gordon and I had lived in the City for a year. Trying to work through the one-way numbered streets was as frustrating now as it had been then.

After we checked into the hotel, I re-energized my batteries, then led the charge down Broadway to Times Square. It was cold and damp, but the heat of the city made the midnight stroll exciting. We had arrived. We had plans to put a week's worth of sightseeing into the next morning. Get ready, New York!

The next morning, Tony couldn't get out of bed. He suffered with ulcers and our midnight adventure had been a bit too much for him. We left him resting. Donna and Gordon accompanied me on a city excursion I had planned. We took the subway to the Staten Island Ferry, boarded and passed the "Lady with the Flame." It was a beautiful morning and she was awesome, rising from the morning mist in New York Harbor.

We took the subway again uptown to the Empire State Building. Donna flicked her camera shutter and I proudly led the way, knowing I was showing her something special. We saw St. Patrick's Cathedral and Rockefeller Center. We did a lot that morning, including crossing streets in heavy traffic. Both Gordon and Donna tried to keep me wedged between them. I wanted to follow the crowd whenever the lights changed. I tried to remember to wait, but there were so many distractions, I couldn't focus. Gordon hung on tight to my hand and Donna died a slow death too. I felt very secure between the two of them. We stopped at a sidewalk "deli" for a quick lunch. We sat and listened to the city fervor as it passed.

By afternoon, Tony had recovered. We dressed and arrived at the theatre for *Miss Saigon* with much excitement. Our seats were magnificent. The show was as great as I knew it would be. I knew the plot thoroughly, and all the songs by heart, word for word. It all came to life that afternoon. As it unfolded, I relived the fight, the loneliness and all the memories. I remembered vividly an earlier time, grey belted in my seat, when I first listened to the words and dreamed of flying. Now, listening to the words, I was mesmerized in my seat, soaring higher than an eagle. How far I had come! This day made the fight worth all the effort. The remainder of the journey would be easier.

That day was the ultimate gift from Gordon to me, and from us to Donna and Tony, and from the music of *Miss Saigon* to all of us.

Both journeys, to New York City and through rehabilitation, had been one of sharing and caring, of helping and support, of love and friendship, of growing and trying the unexpected.

In order to solo, I first had to navigate. I was starting to step forward and beginning to map out the way. But while I was picking up speed, so was Gordon. We were stopped on the ride home, somewhere in Connecticut and given a $190 ticket for speeding.

I reminded him that he had to be sure to "look both ways" before accelerating. I know he wished he had, only sooner. I reached over and held his hand. He recognized it as a signal that I understood how easy it was to forget safety sometimes, and just go.

We came back a little poorer in the pocketbook, but very much richer in other things.

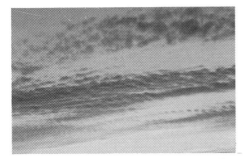

CHAPTER TWENTY ONE

Soloing

By April, I was being left alone at will. I was cleared for safety in the kitchen provided I used the guidelines and strategies I had been taught: always use an apron when cooking to remind me I am not done yet; use timers for the burners and oven; use reminders on the wall and color for focusing and slowing down. My kitchen walls had become decorated with pictures of keys, books, and colors to remind me.

In speech therapy (*Communication Disorders,* as it is called at the hospital), Kathy colored my cue cards neon pink to draw my attention to them. Each time she tried to get me to make proper eye contact or pay attention, she would tap the neon pink card. I began to find my attention drawn to anything neon pink, so much so I would often forget what I was doing and just stare at the whatever the neon pink item was. In my kitchen at home, we had posted neon pink cards to remind me to do certain critical things like turn off stove burners, etc. Sometimes when cooking, if my eye wandered to a card hung near the stove, I would simply forget about cooking. Eventually, I would read the card and follow its directions.

I decided to have my judging scoresheets printed on neon pink paper, thinking this would remind me not to look up from the score sheet until I had finished computing. It would also serve to solve another problem that had developed. If I took my eyes off the scoresheet, I would be unable to look back down and resume the task of calculating. The pink worked and I remembered to always keep focused on the pink.

Gradually as months passed, I found that focusing steadily on anything neon pink in color would make me become more relaxed and calm.

Times when I was totally out of control and unable to solo, my attention to anything neon pink, would help me regain my composure. Usually, I could return to the initial activity.

The hospital had scheduled me to be discharged from physical therapy; however, my occupational therapist was leaving the home health care organization. So the decision was made to continue my physical therapy at New England Rehabilitation Hospital, specifically for community mobility training unavailable through my home care program. My reports showed I checked for approaching traffic 80% of the time. It was the other 20% that concerned everybody.

That was a big improvement, but not what was considered safe.

I still had to have someone with me when I left my home. I was able to go and do many other things by myself. Though I was sure there was always someone nearby for those "other things." But just the knowledge that I was allowed alone "to do it myself," was a sign of continual recovery.

To me, it was the greatest challenge and satisfaction of all.

If time's my greatest healer.
And progress lies in movement.
In spite of all my deficits,
They finally see improvement.

Once I tried and did alone,
And patiently, I learned.
That sometimes, I can't forge ahead,
And leave my bridges burned.

I ask for help to hold me now,
And protect me when I fall.
With no support on which to rest,
There is no ME at all.

Two of my judging colleagues, Marty Butler and Jenny Woodward, and I had planned to drive to Alabama, in April, for the N.C.A.A. Collegiate National Championships in Tuscaloosa. A gymnast from Maine we knew well and had judged through the years as she rose to the Elite level, was competing for the University of Utah. We had seen her the year before at Nationals in Oregon, and had decided to attend this year.

They would take turns driving, while I navigated. I assured them I was very experienced by then, they could relax.

We went via Orlando. Jenny had never been to Disney World and they wanted to lie on the beach a bit and enjoy the night life. I opted to visit my parents for a couple of days. They live in Tavares, only a 30 minute ride north of Orlando. We drove straight through without stopping. It took us 22 hours. Although it rained the whole way down, we met little traffic and had no delays. I did very well navigating. I had help, of course, but the second time navigating was easier than the first.

We left Orlando three days later for Tuscaloosa. The competition was thoroughly enjoyable and Kristen, our gymnast, did a great job, placing fourth all-around in the country.

One of the nights there was a very hot one. The motel room was stifling. We had met Kathy Walley, another colleague, at the airport. She had flown into Birmingham to see the meet. We had four people in our room. The others went to sleep right away. I sat up and listened to music for a while. It was so hot. I decided to open the door to get some air. I realized my friends were asleep and having the door open was sort of exposing them to the outside. I decided to go outside myself.

There was a beautiful breeze blowing. I knew that we had passed a coffee shop down the road. I decided I would walk down and get a cup of coffee. So I put on my earphones and proceeded to do that at 2 a.m. all by myself. Our motel was situated on a very busy six lane highway. I made it, but again I had forgotten to bring any money for the coffee. Luckily, I found some loose change in my pocket. As I sat at a table and was drinking my coffee, Kathy came running down the street. I wondered why she was up. She was supposed to be asleep. I felt badly that I didn't have enough money to even buy her a cup of coffee. I don't think, at that point, she really cared. We walked back together to the motel on a back road that ran parallel to the highway. Kathy thought it was a better idea than walking on the highway. I knew she was afraid we'd get lost, but she didn't know what a good navigator I had become.

It took us about an hour. The road never went back to the hotel. We had to backtrack to the coffee shop and walk to our motel via the highway. We both fell into bed and went right off to sleep. Marty and Jenny never woke up during our adventure. I think Kathy told them later what they had slept through. For the rest of the trip, they made sure I was in bed before them, and the door was locked.

On the way home, we stopped only in Harrisburg, Pennsylvania, for dinner with another colleague. We survived a blizzard in the Poconos, and by the time we arrived in New York, we were all exhausted. But being the navigator, I couldn't sleep. My job was to keep the driver awake. We made it to Portland at 7 a.m.

I was scheduled for out-patient therapy at the hospital later in the day. They dropped me off there in order to save Gordon from having to make two trips to Portland in one day. After calling him to let him know I was back and fine, I dropped my things in the cafeteria.

Just a few minutes later, Donna called from the second floor and asked if I would like an empty bed to lie down on. I could never tell her or anyone else how much that offer meant. I was totally exhausted. I know I was asleep before my head hit the pillow. I never thought there would ever come a time when I would enjoy being in bed at the hospital again. I had been wrong. I slept until they woke me for therapy, much more refreshed.

That day, in speech therapy, we discussed the implications of my nocturnal venture alone. I somehow got the message that I was not yet ready to make judgment decisions regarding my own safety. I needed to think before I acted. I was continuing to improve. Not too long ago, I would not have understood that what I did was dangerous.

I would just have to work harder to remember to slow down and think before attempting to solo in the near future.

That was easier said than done.

CHAPTER TWENTY TWO

Ignition

Sometimes, we need just a little spark to get us going on the right track. It was mid-May, when I was approached by a social worker at the hospital. She asked if I would be interested in talking with another patient who had a head injury similar to mine. I remembered when I had been an in-patient, I had been visited by a *survivor*. She talked with me about what I was experiencing and gave me new ideas and encouragement. I really appreciated and looked forward to her visits. I quickly told the social worker, "Yes."

For the first time, I felt a sense of importance. I had learned how very vital it is that patients with head injury feel needed, to be an active participant in all levels of the recovery process.

I spent time with my new friend and let her know that I understood and was there if she ever wanted to talk.

Other areas were also improving at great strides. I was able to take the bus by myself from the Maine Mall to the city, transfer buses and get to the rehab hospital without supervision. I shopped in busy malls and, though still easily distracted, I was able to continue about my business without getting lost.

When I had to make decisions, like whether to buy one of two items, I would buy them both...or I would have become confused, rushed out of the store and escaped from the choice. I would always write down where the car was, who I had to meet and at what time.

By now, I was aware that the information was always in my right pocket. If I had no pockets, then my book was always there.

I remember one day, doing my weekly grocery shopping at the supermarket. After loading the groceries in the trunk of the car, I went to return the shopping cart. Once back in the store, I simply kept the cart and began to shop all over again. The only way I discovered I had already completed the shopping, was when I checked the list and the items were already crossed off. I still wasn't sure, it wasn't a mistake.

I was now able to go in, shop alone and meet someone at the exit at a specified time. I had come a long way.

Some of the things I had trouble doing, were things that are problems for many people: people often can't remember where they parked the car in a busy Mall parking lot; people have a hard time making decisions; people sometimes screw up recipes when cooking; they forget appointments and telephone calls; they leave irons on and forget to turn the oven off.

When my friends would ask me what specifically my problems were, I found it almost impossible to make them understand. They would say, "God! Bev. You were always like that!"

Unless they had spent a lot of time with me like Marty and Jenny had, they had difficulty understanding the deficits and my compensations. Little things forgotten became major obstacles. As long as I was not tired, there were no decisions, no noise, no stimulation, and no stress, I was doing fine. Add one of the above ingredients, and the whole situation was a different ball game.

I had a problem with some television programs. I could watch the news and take notes. I could listen to the weather and simple movies. I could not stay attentive to programs that used a flashback technique or had multiple story lines in one show, like *Cheers*.

So, during the late spring, my speech therapy included watching a lot of different shows. Kathy and I worked on my sense of humor. I found it difficult to understand jokes. The *Far Side* humor, which I used to enjoy, was totally gone. We used cartoon books in therapy. I practiced trying to understand what I was missing.

My ignition switch seemed to be on delayed start. Each new problem we discovered, we patiently erased as a disability. As we eliminated deficits, my ability to function alone grew and concern for my safety lessened.

Trust was being ignited, and this time it was me that was being trusted. When the staff at New

England Rehab first told me I had to earn everyone's trust, I remembered Dr. Story and his calm and deliberate manner. He earned my trust. I needed to think and do tasks one step at a time, with care, with preplanning and with confidence.

I wasn't sure I could remember all that, but I certainly tried.

One doesn't get very far without turning on the ignition.

TRUSTING THE WIND

Sometimes I have to trust the winds
To find the course to take,
To push me on, or steer me right,
To accelerate or brake.

It isn't always where I go
Or where I think I'm heading.
Sometimes I just need to know
The trajectory I'm getting.

I make body work and sweat
Through sunshine, rain and snow.
The end result is worth the work
When I trust the winds that blow.

There will be ups. There will be downs.
There will be better times to find.
I need to do it by myself
When I've left the winds behind.

No one knows how hard it is
To struggle day to day.
Remembering and forgetting
As I go about my way.

But, one day, I'll venture forth
And blaze a solo track,
Because I learned to trust the winds
To take me there and back.

CHAPTER TWENTY THREE

Trusting the Wind

Head injury victims in recovery face the world as an entry process; totally dependent upon others for cues in behavior, speech and ambulatory skills - much like newborns. There exists that strong, invisible something that connects the successful therapist with the patient, somewhat the same as a mother and child.

In the initial stage of my recovery, consistency and repetition played the largest influence. As I began to internalize the strategies of regular use of my memory book and repeating to myself what was said over and over again, I began to function more independently. I began to feel the need for something else.

I called it *bonding*, the establishment of a connection or trust between two people who have something in common. That something in common was me. It started as a glimmer of hope and then, a sure belief that this person could help me; a trust that they actually would.

In the initial phases of recovery, I was not aware enough of my emotions, so this was not an issue. But as my emotions surfaced and I became more aware of them, I realized I had problems I couldn't solve without the help and support of these people around me. The staff's attempts to get through to me was subtle and carefully planned.

As I worked my way through the rehabilitation, it was the understanding and trust developed with certain therapists that excited my motivation and hastened my improvement. (It is fortunate some therapists are able to instill this. Some patients are not open to the concept of trust.) It really wasn't until much, much later in my recovery that I was able to decipher how my trusting had occurred. Looking back, I now realize this bonding was a vital link in order for me to begin to relearn, focus in and pay attention.

How it came about was different with each therapist. They were never aware that this was happening to me. It was a one-sided bonding, but that was all that was necessary for me to listen and actually believe in what they said. That was the key! It was sort of like trusting, just for a moment, while the learning takes place; then the trust recedes, leaving only the learning. I liken it to trusting the wind and letting it blow you over the earth to reseed, nurture and begin to grow again.

Donna and Tony

Donna was the first to "make the connection" with me. She was about my age and married to Tony, the lab technician at the hospital. (They were the couple in the earlier chapters who went to New York with Gordon and I) Tony was a baseball umpire. He would stop during his rounds in the hall and kid me about my gymnastics judging. I liked him, we had something in common.

I had been very excited about the impending birth of my third grandchild. Having two grandsons, I don't know who wanted a girl more, my daughter or myself. When the news arrived that I had a new granddaughter, I couldn't wait to see her.

When she was about ten days old, the whole family came for a visit. I carried around Jessica Marie, so all the patients could see my pride and joy. I talked to her as I cuddled my grandsons and shared the excitement of my world with them. They were intrigued by the workings of the wheelchair, my casts and the bed that went up and down.

Later, we went out on the patio to enjoy each other's company. The boys began to run around. I had trouble coping with the commotion and suddenly, needed to get away. I turned and re-entered the cafeteria. But by then, the nurses were eating lunch and inquired where I was going alone. I retreated silently back to the patio. The rest of my family were talking together and were totally unaware that anything was wrong. I think I was just about to run in panic, in the other direction toward the street, when Donna came up behind me and put her hand on my shoulder. As I turned, she said, "Would you like me to take you to your room to rest for awhile?"

I didn't know how she knew what I needed. But I said, "Yes."

She escorted me to my room, put me into bed and turned out the lights.

I deeply love my family. I had waited a long time for my grandchildren to visit. But my brain wasn't able to sort out the confusion and deal with the over-stimulation. Donna returned to the patio and explained to my family what had just happened. They would have to wait for awhile and after a rest, I would be OK. My husband understood. I'm not sure that my daughter ever did.

After that day, I trusted Donna to help me. Like Dr. Story, she had taken control when I was unable, and that strength reached me. Because of that inner feeling of trust I felt for Donna, she was able to get through to me when I needed to focus in on safety, and concentrate on listening to her. Donna was someone special and I felt safe with her around. She knew what I needed before I knew myself. She never got excited and never raised her voice. She was the calm person that I used to be, and I could identify with that. She was very gentle. I liked gentle people. There was obviously a deep love between she and her husband. They also worked together in the same building. I had worked for eight years in the same building with my husband and I loved him dearly. I saw the similarities I had with her. Beyond the similarities, I trusted and respected her.

Trisha

My bonding with Trisha, my physical therapist, was built one day during a therapy session as she literally crept on her hands and knees, up and down the entire first floor corridor. As I tried to walk, she crept beside me carefully placing my foot in the proper position with each step. She worked patiently for an hour, determined to help me try to feel where my foot was and where I had to put it. I felt so sorry for her as we worked our way, back and forth, up and down the corridor. I knew that she was special and she cared. I knew I had to exert extra energy to try and help her.

She cared enough to take whatever time was necessary to see that I improved. She was patient, persistent and gave me the motivation I needed to keep trying.

I liked Trisha and after that day, I knew she cared about me and my recovery. Unfortunately for Trisha, as I became more sure of myself and able to walk on my own, she learned not to return my trust. She would take me for daily walks through the halls of the hospital and try to get me lost. Little did she know, I knew the hospital as well as she did. Sometimes, something just happened in my brain, and I lost my awareness of where I was. But, at other times, I silently became an appendage of the "medical octopus." Our day trips became my scouting trips for late night on-my-own exploration. I loved physical therapy and everything about it. I trusted Trisha. She was the first to take me outdoors around the promenade. She tried to get me lost during walks together in the surrounding community. She did. But I always had faith, throughout my rehabilitation, that Trisha would do whatever I needed to have done to improve...and she did...and I did.

Sarah

Sarah, my out-patient physical therapist, had heard of my exploits before she inherited me from Trisha. She was ready for me. Everything Sarah did was pre-planned, planned and re-planned. But she learned to be surprised and I even think, frightened with me, as I learned to trust her.

Together, we faced the unexpected. I would constantly do what she didn't expect. Much of her therapy had been geared to help me recognize the weaknesses in my leg and foot and compensate. It was hard for me to do that. Later as I resumed judging higher-level collegiate meets, I felt conspicuous being confined to sneakers and a brace. I tried wearing heels a couple of times and almost killed myself. Sarah found out and tried to make me understand how dangerous that was. When I couldn't promise her that I wouldn't do it again, she had talks with my colleagues, to see that I couldn't and didn't.

Sarah was soft-spoken and tiny, but she was certainly no pushover. She had been as determined to see I met with success as I was.

I bonded to Sarah during times of panic, either hers or mine, and there was plenty of both. She would get angry with me and let me know when I had used bad judgment. I got frustrated in my other therapies, but in physical therapy, I also became frightened. There were many opportunities to do myself physical harm because I couldn't realize the potential danger of a given situation. Sarah would work out compensations for me to try. We would identify my physical impairment and go from there.

At one point late in my out-patient therapy, after an ordered O.T. evaluation, I was scheduled by the evaluator for a group therapy in assertiveness. Unfortunately, I had a panic attack in the first session. It was a very cold day back in February. I bolted from the room and building in a state of sheer panic. I had on slacks and only a short-sleeved blouse. Luckily, I had my earphones on, or I could still be out there today. I remember wandering on the main street and trying to get on the Transit Bus at the Maine Medical Center, but the driver wouldn't let me on. I had no money.

The realization that I had no money panicked me even more. I was so cold. I knew I needed a jacket. I didn't know where to get a jacket and I had no money. But why didn't I have money? I wasn't poor?

The next clear recollection is standing in front of Sarah, back at the hospital, hysterical. I must have sought her out because I trusted her to help me. I was crying, freezing, totally hysterical, and had no idea where I belonged.

She returned me to my therapy session. When she opened the door, I saw my jacket, pocketbook and memory book on the floor beside a chair and I calmed down. I managed to warm up and recover a part of myself, quietly. The therapist of the session was Carolyn, my old swim therapist. That was the end of my assertiveness therapy. Poor Carolyn! She lost me again. My support team pulled me out of class that afternoon. They said I was not ready for it yet. They were probably right.

Dr. Oliverio

I was subsequently assigned to attend coping classes of the pain management therapy group at the hospital. It was a much more guarded program with Dr. Oliverio. They felt that if I panicked here, she could maintain control. I had been in a group session of hers before I was discharged as an in-patient. I don't remember ever saying anything or contributing anything during those sessions.

One day, as I was approaching my discharge, she turned and said, "It's scary to go home, isn't it, Beverley."

I remember I looked at her in utter shock and wondered how, on earth, she knew what I was thinking. I never forgot those words. Somehow, she knew I was scared, even before I recognized it. It was a long time before I realized that those simple words had developed a bonding with Dr. Oliverio. Those words that day, built a trust for me that she knew what I was experiencing and understood. I didn't have to tell her...it was automatic, like fish on Friday nights...like shit happens...like getting excited at Super Bowls...like sunshine always follows the rain. She just knew!

Rita Oliverio, the counseling psychologist, is a tall, stately, Penn State Graduate with an extremely calming voice, who swiftly became a strong, calming force and took control of the situation. I trusted her, like I had Dr. Story. I knew she would make the best decisions, if I suddenly had a problem. I left a couple of times in panic again, but regained my composure and returned quickly. I felt secure with her around.

Those sessions did more to develop my sense of confidence for me than any other. I listened. I tuned in. I tried to pay attention. I talked little, but I heard and I watched and I learned from others. It was a long time before I was able to join in the discussion. There were times when I cried, and when she touched me, I knew she understood.

Gradually, I lost the need to run. Oh, the need was still there, but with her help, I learned to stay put. Her questions seemed to reach down to the depths of my soul and pull out all the plugs. As the pain group changed from month to month, I remained. With my head injury, I needed the repetition of hearing the same thing over and over. The repetition began to have an effect on me. I slowly began to absorb the lectures and very gradually, they began to make sense to me. Each month I became stronger. Slowly and gradually, part of me drained away. What remained was much stronger and more potent than before. I felt like I was very slowly becoming an aged wine from Oliverio's distillery.

She probably will never know how important she was to my eventual recovery...and perhaps, it is best leaving it that way. We need to talk out and solve our own problems and anger, and write books, if need be. Good psychologists probably understand that better than anyone else.

We need to believe in our own inner strength and "trusting the winds" will follow. I wonder how many other people recovering from brain injury are first reached though this trusting. I have learned that it is not only a key ingredient in the beginning process of recovery, but continues just as strong, if not even stronger, in the ending phases of recovery.

It's a natural process. The first thing we do in life when we need help. It certainly is a powerful beginning. No wonder God reserved this special kind of bonding for mother and child.

 *Accelerating*

In June, I was On-Site Director for the National Association of Women's Gymnastics Judges' National Symposium held at the Sheraton-Tara in South Portland. This symposium is held every two years and it had never been in the eastern part of the United States.

Everybody at the last one, in Costa Mesa in southern California, was very excited to finally be coming to the East. We were also excited in Maine about having the opportunity to be the host state.

It was a tremendous undertaking for states the size of California, Colorado, and New York, who had hundreds of judges to volunteer for committees. Maine had only about 20 judges on its roster.

That meant every person had to do many jobs.

I didn't know if it was even possible for us to pull it off. Since I was a well known National judge, a lot of pressure rested on my shoulders to carry it through and do a credible job. The rest of the Region and the East were banking on a super symposium.

Marty Butler, who had taken over my former job as State Judging Director, took charge of the advance printing and mailings, scheduling workers and volunteers, and the registration table.

I took charge of the banquet entertainment, scheduling of the rooms for different sessions, audio visual equipment rental, a cruise and lobster bake, and ground transportation.

Our job would be to work with The National Symposium Director from Wisconsin. Since she was there and we were here, we knew most of the work would be ours to do. She was responsible for the clinicians, hotel and budget.

During early June, I was overwhelmed with the volume of work that needed to be done. Marty had a very demanding full time job, and I was still in physical therapy and speech therapy two days a week.

When I first mentioned to my therapists that I was involved in this undertaking, they had no idea of the enormity of the task. As we started to discuss the symposium in detail and the amount of responsibilities on me, they recognized the insecurity I could only allow to surface behind the privacy of therapy doors.

My colleagues had to believe I was sure we could do it, or their confidence might be undermined.

My speech therapist wanted me to reconsider. She knew that it was much too much of a job for me to take on so soon. I have to admit now, I did too. But I had committed myself two years before and knew full well, if I had not guaranteed the National Director I'd personally do it, we would not have been awarded the host site.

Even though there were extenuating circumstances, I could not let them down. I had given my word and my word was known to be good.

My speech therapist was unable to talk me out of my commitment. So she did the next best thing. She chipped in and helped me break down the complex tasks into smaller steps I could handle.

She helped me build a time frame in which to complete certain tasks, and made sure I accomplished each of them.

It would also be the first time I would see many of my colleagues from around the country since my accident. In addition to all the stress of responsibility for this undertaking, I was also concerned about their reaction to my injury.

On top of everything else, a few weeks before the Convention began, I received a call from our country's "top" clinician. She had received a copy from the National Governing Board of a letter I had written to the National Certification Chairman eight months before, about my hospitalization, injury and my attempt to "Hang In There."

The theme of the national symposium was *Hanging In There* and she wanted to read my letter at the opening session. She asked me to take part in the opening session and discuss my recuperation - in front of 300 of my national colleagues. Hopefully, my motivation to "hang in there" would encourage them to keep trying when their roads seemed rough.

The letter was more personal than I wanted to share publicly, but I was unable to refuse her request. In fact, learning to say 'No' was a response that I was frantically trying to learn in therapy.

I was not ready to deal yet with this much pressure and did not know how I would react. What if I ran? I was still having problems functioning in small groups and would suddenly bolt out of the room, if anyone put pressure on me.

But I knew, I needed to try. I could not admit to my colleagues I wasn't able to do it. I would just pray I didn't fail. If I did, I knew my credibility as a judge was lost. I knew at some time, I would have to face this fear head-on.

But first I needed to tend to all the other incidentals: the audio visual rentals, lecture room set ups, side trips, a cruise and lobster bake for 130, banquet tickets for 300, luncheon tickets, copying lecture information, getting people to different places and nearby clinics (even though I couldn't drive).

Worst of all, writing a banquet entertainment program that would keep the audience laughing and leave them with fond memories to take home.

That was a job no one else on ANY level wanted to do.

It took me forever to write the script for the entertainment. Everyday when I returned to the computer to continue the story line, I had to reread the entire script because I couldn't remember what I had written the day before.

I learned to take things as they came. In order to be productive, I had to become patient. I could not function like I had before.

My colleagues from Maine did a superb job getting everything ready and staffing the registration tables. Working together, they did everything anyone could have expected of them and more.

They drove, guided, gave advice, and became friends with all the registrants. They were the good will ambassadors for the State of Maine and the East.

My support team stayed with me throughout the week. My daughter made a video of all the week's activities, cut and edited a sound track into the video to make a movie. She also recorded segments of 26 tapes of sound effects for the script, and then, ran the sound system for the show.

My husband did the videotaping of the actual performance and served as a "gofer" for whatever I had forgotten.

Staff from the rehabilitation hospital volunteered to come and do anything I needed to have done. I really appreciated their offers, but most of the work had to be done by us. However, Tony and Donna, along with Lorraine, the secretary on the head injury wing, ran a spotlight for the show. It took a lot of their own time, but they never once complained amidst the confusion.

I'm sure now that they were there for my benefit. They knew nothing about spotlights and everything about me. They gave their own time to volunteer with me throughout the week, in case I needed their help.........and yes, occasionally, I did.

I knew I could trust them. They knew I was approaching my limits before I knew myself. When I reached those limits, we escaped together. Those were the periods I was unable to share with my colleagues and friends.

A difficult time for me, was when I left the hustle and bustle of the hotel to go to a therapy session. I was OK and functioning when in the confusion of the symposium registration. Once in the peace and quiet of the hospital, I totally lost control. I had no intentions of returning. I began to cry and once I did, I was unable to deal with what had been happening. I'm sure that without the patience of many staff, I would have disappeared into oblivion - A.W.O.L.

The night of dress rehearsal for our banquet skit was a night of surprises. We had overrun our time in the banquet hall. We were keeping the help overtime. We had rehearsed less than a quarter of the script in our allotted time. Characters did not know their lines or roles. (I had directed different high school productions, involving hundreds of teenagers, and none of them had ever been this bad.) Nothing was going as planned.

I was incapable of dealing with anything more. A colleague came into the dining room to inform us that we needed to provide several drivers to start a tour to L.L.Beans that was 10 minutes late. The leads in the show were all pre-assigned drivers.

I "lost it," to say the least.

I don't remember how I left, but suddenly I found myself in the middle of the hotel parking lot. I don't remember anything except Donna (my nurse left her spotlight) holding me tightly and telling me over and over, "Look at my shirt." Needless to say, her shirt was neon pink. I don't recall how long we were there.

When I returned to the rehearsal, other judges had taken over for me and were doing fine, much better than I.

I had to leave once more, before I could get myself back on track. But, I returned to finish what I had worked so hard for, and my colleagues understood.

Donna felt I shouldn't be alone in the hotel room that night. She strongly suggested I go home with her and she would return me by 7 a.m. the next morning, before anyone would miss me.

I had learned to accept one fact as inevitable during my recovery and that was, Donna Levesque was always right. Don't ask why. Just follow directions.

Even believing that, I did not go quietly or easily. I returned in the morning refreshed and ready to start again.

The judges from Maine and New Hampshire performed the 90 minute show that brought down the house. They did a fabulous job.

By all of us working together, we made it. The symposium was a great success, the best ever. That was the opinion expressed by everyone there. Letters of congratulations rolled in for months after it was over.

Personally, I did not have time to talk much with my old friends. But after the opening session, there wasn't really the need. I didn't run. There were times when I felt I needed to, but I ground my feet into the floor, breathed deeply and tried to think of other things. The audience gave me a standing ovation. I told them it really belonged to my support team. Without them, the symposium could not have been successful. I knew that was a fact.

In July, the National Office called to ask if they could publish my original letter in the National

Newsletter as an inspiration to those judges across the country who were unable to attend the symposium. I agreed. This time I no longer worried about what people would think.

The Conference wasn't just a victory for me. I knew it was a victory for all the "little" states. The states who never get a chance to prove they can do it as well as the big ones. I felt good for having been a part of it.

I felt it was also a victory for all people with head injury. To never admit that something can't be done is worth its weight in gold. I learned that when people say you can't do something, that's the time to stand up and demand OF yourself and FOR yourself, nothing less than total victory.

Sometimes we don't get a chance to get patted on the back for trying. I was one of the lucky ones. I had. It made it all worth while.

Donna, Tony and Lorraine tried something new they would never have had the opportunity to do otherwise. They had gone that extra mile to work with a patient as a friend in the process.

By working together, we found our space to fly. We all even flew a little higher that June summer night... in search of wings.

LETTING GO

The hardest thing that I have found
for my family to know
is when to closely hang on tight
and when to let me go.

It is a judgment hard to make
for all those in command.
Whether to let me try alone
to see if I can stand.

Therapists have the same task
as they help me try to move.
I try to do all that they ask
and do things they approve.

But there always comes a time
when I need to test my will.
I need to step beyond the fence
and climb another hill.

Although it's been a long time
I want to start today.
no one is sure I'll make it
or if I will lose my way.

It's hard for them to back off and
let me try, 'cause then
if I should fall and hurt myself
we'd have to start again.

Sometimes we need to let love go
and stumble through the tears.
I will learn from all the struggle.
I will grow from all the fears.

And if, by chance, I lose the way
I'll treat myself with care.
I'll cherish every tiny step
I used to get me there.

It's an art to know that turning point
that determines when they know
If they need to keep hanging on to me
or step back and let me go.

CHAPTER TWENTY FIVE

Cleared For Take-off

One of my three goals was to be able to fly alone. I stated this emphatically at my September family conference. It was decided, against my better judgment, that if I needed to fly, I must have someone with me. It was felt my distractibility was still an unresolved problem. I knew unless they allowed me that chance to try, I'd never know for sure. I needed to know.

Gordon and I took a trip to England and Scotland. When we left, he knew he had to keep an extra eye out for me. I was sure, as always, I could take care of myself.

We met our son, Mark, and his fiance at the airport, and left London on a 1500 mile car jaunt to and throughout Scotland. We had a joyous trip.

I was mesmerized by the beautiful countryside and friendly people.

No one had to remind me to use my memory book. It was my record of the places we'd been and the things we did. I didn't care that it was still necessary for me to use it. I wanted to remember everything...and I knew my book would allow me to do that.

We went directly to Edinburgh where I'm ashamed to admit, I almost got killed re-learning lesson #1, "Look both ways." I did look before crossing the street, but since they drive on the other side of the road, I looked the wrong way. As I stepped out, a car came so close to my leg that it ripped the leg of my slacks.

My husband yelled my name and I ran - toward the other side. WRONG! A normal reaction would probably have been to stop or step back. My reaction was instinctive; flee from the danger. But I panicked, and just ran across the intersection without thinking.

It was vital to all our sanity that we immediately stop and talk about my reaction, and how we would compensate and adjust. Gordon kept his hand in mine at every crosswalk for the next two weeks. He rested better and I felt safe.

We traveled to Pitlochry, toured castles, drove north through the highlands, and down along the lush hills to the quaint village of Drumnadrochit. We cruised on Loch Ness where I half-heartedly searched in vain for Nessie. The truth is I prayed, that if there was such a thing as a monster, it didn't show up while I was there. Because of my head injury, no one would ever believe me.

We bed and breakfasted on the Isle of Skye, shopped in Collander, and rested in the village of Luss, on the shore of Loch Lomond. It was more beautiful than I had ever imagined.

I enjoyed the absence of a schedule, of always being in a hurry. We spent the days as we wanted.

Seven days later we ended up in Bath, England. The following morning, we travelled by train to London where we remained for several days, shopped and rested. We saw *Phantom of the Opera* at Her Majesty's Theatre and *Miss Saigon* at Drury Lane. I had always loved the theatre. Since we had seen both shows in New York on Broadway, we compared casts and productions. I felt the same closeness to the music in London that I had felt while in the hospital.

I made sure each day was safely preserved in my memory book. It included things I did, that I shouldn't have done, as well as things I didn't do, that I should have. Later I would find ways to correct those areas that still needed help.

I practiced my strategies in the hustle and bustle of Picadilly Circus. I found that other than shopping in several stores a second and third time without knowing it, I was surviving well. It only hurt the purse.

I also realized how fortunate we were to be blessed with the opportunity to do these things. Many people at home might never have this opportunity. That made me want to absorb and retain all the more.

We returned to Boston on September 5, late in the evening and travelled the 150 miles north to our home. It was after midnight by the time we arrived.

I spent the early morning hours laundering my clothes from the trip and repacking them into my luggage to go again. I opened all the mail needing attention and wrote checks for the most important of the inevitable bills that had accumulated while we were gone. I didn't function well when I was tired. I was exhausted.

At 5 a.m. Gordon and I set out for the Portland Jetport so that I could take to the skies again on a 7 a.m. flight to Indianapolis.

This time, I was headed to the World Gymnastics Championships. I was travelling with several of my colleagues. They would be there, if I needed them, but I would be trying to make the trip on my own. I purposely did not volunteer to work at the meet, so I could practice being responsible for myself.

I heard the uneasiness with which Gordon said, "Goodby. Be careful." at the departure gate.

But I had plans to fulfill and a journey to continue. I knew he understood.

There was no special schedule. There was plenty of confusion, immense crowds, much traffic, walking on my own, and decision-making. Other than being much too tired, which was totally understandable, I managed quite well. One day when I found myself in need of getting away from everything, I took a cab from the hotel to a university library nearby. It turned out to be a perfect place to take a time-out and recoup. It was very quiet and I could find plenty to do.

I was pleased I didn't have to ask for help from my friends. They were careful to keep an eye on me. It was now more for their own satisfaction than my safety. The competition was excellent. The U.S.A. won a silver medal in the women's team competition. We had never earned a medal before in the team competition. Our leading gymnast also took the all-around gold medal. I had difficulty staying focused on the competition, in spite of the good seats and the excitement. But I could deal with that as trivial, compared to the past year.

Although it was a once in a lifetime experience to view the world championships up close, I found myself bored. I'm not sure which was worse, the boredom or the exhaustion. I know my trip bordered on the edge of each. I returned home 10 days later to a very appreciative husband, a month's work of unfinished business and a huge cardboard box overflowing with unopened mail. I spent the next day working on all three.

The second day home, I discovered that I had a free flight from United Airlines that had to be used by October 1, (only two weeks away) or forfeited.

I don't like to lose free trips. One of my three goals was to travel ALONE on planes. Even though Dr. Caldwell had said this was not possible and not recommended, would Gordon consent to let me try?

We decided that I could use the ticket to fly to Orlando to visit my parents. They had not been able to come North during the summer and would be thrilled if I visited them again. Gordon agreed I could attempt it, provided I didn't surprise them. I would have to let them know I was coming. I wanted to make it a surprise, but could understand why that was not practical. They would meet me at the airport. My flight left the next morning.

My ticket showed I would have to change planes in Washington, D.C. I had done that many times before and was familiar with the procedure.

I felt confident I would encounter no problems I couldn't handle. This was my chance to show that I could travel by myself.

The biggest challenge would be the fatigue left over from my trip to the World Competition. It had only been two days and I had not rested much. I also knew that when I was tired, my deficits seem to multiply.

I finished paying the bills and mortgages, recording rent payments and posting ledgers. I did the laundry and repacked my suitcase.

At 5 a.m. the next morning, we headed out again for the airport. I was about to earn my wings and I couldn't wait.

Even though I planned what I would do, upon disembarking in Washington D.C., I encountered a problem. I needed to change from Terminal B to Terminal C. I had done this many times before.

Even though I am not a follower by nature, I somehow followed the crowd to the baggage claim area. When my bags didn't arrive on the carousel, I didn't worry or panic. I knew what to do. I attempted to file a lost baggage report. A baggage claim attendant checked my tickets and told me I was going onto Orlando. I became indignant. I said, "I know that!"

When he then said I was only in Washington. I became even more indignant. I said, "I know that, too."

"Well, lady," he said, "your bags are headed for Orlando and you should be too."

BINGO! The light dawned. I realized what I had done. Instantly heart pounds...Oh God!....Where am I supposed to be...I've done it again.

Luckily, I had a ninety minute layover or I would have missed my connecting flight. I learned a valuable lesson. I was still very susceptible to losing my focus, my direction. I was still so easily distracted. However, I managed to complete my flight as scheduled.

My parents were thrilled and very relieved when I came through the arrival gate in Orlando. They had been more nervous than I about me getting there safely.

No one thought I could do it and I did it. I was on a roll. However, on the return flight, I was taking no chances.

Since I only had a 20 minute layover, I decided to not even go to the ladies room, in fear that I would get distracted and miss my flight.

I learned. We all learn.

I just learn a little slower.

I know I will rest before I venture forth alone again. But earning my wings to fly alone, was worth the gamble and the reward.

I know I must still pay attention and stay focused on the task at hand. It is vital that I hold my head up and set out straight ahead in my search for those other wings...the most important ones, that let us fly above the obstacles and move on with life.

I know they can't be far away.

WINGS

When I endure hard times, and can't understand why.
I think of an eagle, just learning to fly.

How high it can soar, and how fast it will glide.
I know that the journey's worth more than the ride.

Sometimes my arms ache, and I want to stop trying,
because it hurts so much, just to keep on flying.

But I've just begun soaring, looking over my realm.
Conquering the obstacles, and taking the helm.

This world could be mine. I just have to believe it.
My wings are my strength, I just have to perceive it.

So when my body won't work, like I want it to
I think of the beautiful things eagles do.

I envision their journey and how high I could soar.
If I'd just spread my wings, and try it once more.

When the going gets tough, and I want to rest longer.
I think of my wings getting stronger and stronger.

Relearning to trust, is related to flying.
Relearning to fly, is related to trying.

When they tell me, I can't; I know that I must.
Pull in my wings, and remember to trust.

For the trusting breeds faith, that carries me to it
By trying once more, when I knew I could do it.

In Search of Wings

CHAPTER TWENTY SIX

Co-Piloting

By October, I was preparing for my discharge from speech therapy. My support team decided it would be good experience for me as well as good therapy to do volunteer work at the hospital. There, they could watch me in a work situation that would be distractible, yet controlled. I would have a chance to do things I felt comfortable doing, and they could pinpoint exact areas needing additional attention.

I thought that was a terrific idea, and was looking forward to the opportunity. I loved to help others. Perhaps it was instinctive. I'd like to think so. A head injury does not change the natural desire to be part of what's happening in one's immediate environment. My support team had doubts about most of the things I thought I wanted to try. I was soon to find out why! Trying to put someone with deficits in judgment, combined with distractibility, on a task was an interesting dilemma.

TRIAL AND ERROR

I'm glad I'm not a goldfish,
And let me tell you why.
When they start to wobble,
They are "flushed" away to die.

Maybe with a little love,
They could once more swim away.
But when they lean upon their side,
We're quick to "flush" away.

It happened fast and one was gone.
T'was better if it drowned.
The only thing that gave concern,
Was who would "flush" it down.

When I look at goldfish now,
I have that gnawing doubt.
That unless I hold my head up,
The world will "flush" me out.

I remember one time I volunteered while still an in-patient. It was something I shouldn't have done, but didn't realize it.

I was sitting in my wheelchair in the hall next to another patient, Mel, a retired lobsterman who had suffered a stroke. He was straight-forward with whatever he said, and like most men who made their life from the sea, he gave no quarter and asked none. My father-in-law had been a lobsterman. I liked Mel. Maybe because he reminded me of my own family. I liked people who told it like it was.

Suddenly, Mel began to talk to a nurse who wasn't there. He wanted to be taken back to his room. He kept saying it over and over, each time more exasperated and louder than before. When the nurse returned, I told her Mel wanted to go to his room. She was very busy and smiled. She said she would take him just as soon as she finished what she was doing. I didn't think she understood that Mel wanted to go NOW.

So after she left the area, I turned and said, "Don't worry, Mel. I can take you."

Mel looked over at me and said "Good."

As I wheeled him down the corridor, someone I passed said that he belonged in Room 213 in the bed next to the sink. I thought, "Oh my God, Mel has to sleep in the bathroom. Poor Guy."

I had a private room with a private bath and had no idea that other patients' rooms were not like mine. When I arrived in 213, I saw the sink and wheeled Mel up to the bed nearest it. I was relieved to know he didn't have to sleep in the bathroom. I started to think about which way to turn his wheelchair before I left, then I remembered the words, "He goes in the bed next to the sink."

Of course! This was a test for me to see if I could listen, understand directions and follow through safely. This staff was not about to fool me. I knew more than they thought I did. I would surprise them.

I had no doubt Mel trusted me too. I was sure this was a test, planned by the nurses, to see if I could make proper decisions on my own without any help or reminders. I knew I could. I told Mel I was going to put him in bed. He looked up and said, "Good!"

In Search of Wings

I tried to think of what to do first. He had a brace on his arm and I knew he didn't wear that in bed. I had to take it off. So I figured out how to undo it and took it apart, piece by piece. I neatly placed all the parts on the sink counter. I was proud of how I figured it out. The staff would be pleased with how carefully I was doing this.

I knew ABSOLUTELY I had to lock his wheelchair in place, so it could not move. Not doing that would be very dangerous! The staff had certainly instilled that knowledge in me. This was a test to see if I knew that - and I knew that.

After everything was complete, I told Mel I was going to lift him up. I had watched the therapists carefully and knew they put their arms around the patient and hung onto the back of their pants to lift them. I wasn't sure I could lift Mel, but I wasn't stupid. They never would have let me get into this situation, if they didn't think I couldn't do it. I looked down at Mel and said "OK. Here we go."

I lifted Mel to a half-standing position, for about four seconds. There was this sudden, tremendous dead weight pulling me over the side of his wheelchair. His weak left side and my weak right side, facing each other, brought disastrous results. I never let go of him though. The wheelchair crashed first. Then I plunged over the wheelchair and plummeted to the floor. Mel came down on top of me.

I thought, at first, I was dead. Worse though, I was scared Mel was dead. Just as I looked up at him, he opened his mouth and mumbled something. I never knew what he said, but I don't think it was "Good."

I saw the nurse's button dangling near me beside the bed. I knew I should push it, but I didn't want anyone to see us like this. But I couldn't move. I don't know if I pushed it or not, but seconds later several nurses ran into the room, followed by the whole second floor staff.

They took one look at us on the floor. Then, I wished I was dead. I think I managed to tell Karen, one of the floor staff, that I had dropped Mel. From then on, I don't remember too much. I know the tears started and I wanted to tell everybody that I was only trying to help. I didn't need to be told to go to my room. Being hysterical, I couldn't wait to get there. The thought that I might have injured Mel in my first attempt to help someone was frightening. To know that I had just flunked their test was humiliating.

The neuropsychologist was in my room practically before I was. It was a long wait for him and words of reassurance before I emerged from under my pillow. It took hours for the tears to subside and a day or so to recuperate from the failure. My body took a lot longer to lose the black and blues.

The next morning Mel and I were together again in the hall. He asked again for someone to take him to his room. I turned toward him and said, "Well, It's not going to be ME."

He turned to me and said, "Good."

In spite of his word, I don't think he remembered what had happened. But I always felt closer to Mel after that day, "on the floor."

It had been 13 months since that day, and they'd just let me officially start to volunteer again. My job was in the medical records department. My assigned task was to cross-check from the hospital list and put deceased stickers on the patients' files.

I allowed myself to cry again that day for Mel... one last time...when I came to his name. He and I shared something special.

Helping Others

At first, I was assigned to volunteer in jobs where I was not distracted and could easily stay focused, like my work in the medical records department. I was given simple tasks with a high degree of repetitiveness to them. When I succeeded at doing those tasks, I was given others demanding some initiative and organization. These were much harder for me. If distracted, I would forget what my goal was.

My first task was to reorganize the contents of the speech department's large storage cabinet. Kathy took me down the day before I was scheduled to start, and showed it to me. When she opened the doors, it did not look salvageable. It closely resembled the remnants of a birthday party for hyperactive five year olds.

I knew then the speech department was a busy one. She told me I would have to organize and relabel the shelves, and their contents. I could see it was going to be a formidable chore. But I felt a "here comes superwoman to the rescue" kind of motivation, and assured her, I would have no problem.

On Thursday I arrived, as scheduled, ready and willing to attack the cabinet. I went directly to the O.T. Room, with all the therapists milling around, said "Good morning" to everybody.

I swung open the cabinet doors to begin. As I looked into the closet and leaned against the open doors with both arms, my heart started to pound. I was faced with the sense of inevitable doom that overwhelms people in panic attacks. I knew I had to get out of there. But my feet wouldn't move. I tried breathing deeply. I squeezed both doors tight around my ears so no one in the room would know I was in an escape mode. The more I tried to stay calm and look at the closet, the more confused and panicked I became. The tears started to roll down my cheeks and I squeezed the doors even tighter around my ears, to hide in the privacy between the closet doors. Each time I opened my eyes to survey the task, my brain became more confused and the tears flowed harder.

All of a sudden, I felt a hand on my back and a soothing voice saying, "Hi Bev, What are you doing in the closet?"

I turned without thinking. It was Elaine, a staff member in quality utilization. She immediately recognized I was in need of quick repair. I could only whisper to her that I didn't know where to start. She was not only friendly, but understood immediately the help I needed. She said softly, "Why don't we do just one shelf at a time."

She suggested that we start with the top one. We could get an adjustable table from one of the patient's rooms and put it under the shelf I was working on, so that I did not get distracted and confused by the other shelves. I hung up neon pink strips of ribbon on the inside of each door to help me stay focused within the cabinet. I finished the closet that day. It was not an easy job. It was a very challenging one for me. I needed challenges. I also knew I would have lost a very valuable piece of confidence in my search for wings, had it not been for Elaine. She was not a scheduled part of my therapy, but without her that day, a closet that had undergone the internal ravaging of war, would not have received justice.

I realized that day that rehabilitation involves not just the support team that works with each person, but the whole staff working together. Each one of my other volunteer jobs was different. I learned to use the copier which sat in the front lobby. My job was to copy information for various departments and staff members. It was a good test against distractibility because of the location of the copier. Most of my paperwork also involved filing and alphabetizing, which still was hard for me.

Helping Myself

I was assigned therapy at the hospital with Dr. Marks, a neuropsychologist, to deal with some of my specific deficits. It was determined I should re-learn to "scan the environment" in order to help prepare me for driving again. I wanted badly to return to driving and was willing to try whatever they thought appropriate in order to get my license again. In order to test and utilize my scanning technique in a controlled situation, I was assigned to horseback riding therapy. I would practice new strategies, try to scan without becoming focused on one thing. My therapy was designed to provide opportunities to help me stay focused on a particular task without being distracted. Yet, I also had to be aware of what was happening around me, without becoming focused on any one thing. We used various techniques for my attention deficits.

Another of my jobs was a "Side-walker." Meant to increase my endurance, I was assigned to walk beside the horse with another patient astride. I had to walk the horse in a particular direction and watch the patient's foot in the stirrup. I would visualize the rider's posture in relation to the horse and then my body in relation to the lines of the horse while we walked. I about drove myself crazy and, of course, wore myself out. As I gained more endurance, I would remember to pay attention to the patient. Though there was improvement over the three months I worked with the horses, we never quite reached the level we had hoped. It was good practice for driving because we were in an outdoor ring with plenty of distractions. I was responsible for my own safety as well as someone else's. My decisions affected not only me, but another human being.

Another valuable tool vital to my rehabilitation was my computer. I purchased attention training software to practice at home each day. I used software to help me stay focused and deal with distractions. Dr. Marks suggested that I play Nintendo in order to improve my concentration and eye/hand coordination.

By December, he wanted me to invest in driving simulation software. It needed to have plenty of distractions. The more, the better. I should use the software as often as possible and keep track of my progress. I found myself attracted to all of the driving games at arcades, theatres and malls.

It was great therapy. Not because of its uniqueness, but because I could see my progress as I continued to work the program. Each day I knew what I had done wrong and also knew what I had to do to improve. Gordon saw to it that I diligently spent at least an hour every day playing Dr. Mario® with him.

We were trying new and experimental therapies to get me back to the point where I could live with myself and my limitations. Not being able to drive was difficult to accept. (It is discussed in more detail in the next chapter.)

Helping others and volunteering helped restore a sense of self-worth, and served as a prelude to the art of being able to help myself once again. That's a good enough reason for anyone, with or without injury, to spend time helping others. I would work on my own recovery while I delivered patients' mail, held their hands, gave them words of encouragement, or helped transport them to another floor. I knew how they felt and anything I could do to make their recovery easier to bear, was worth my time and effort. We all need others for inner strength.

While I was helping them, they were helping me even more.

Co-Piloting is a skill we all must learn. To lend confidence by our presence, to lend reassurance in times of concern, to be companions to those who need us; these are parts of life we need to nurture and hold precious.

SHARING THE HEALING

I was once the "healing,"
Locked with my chair.
And when I found I needed help,
There was always someone there.

I hear the "healing" start to sing.
I know the song, but then. . .
This time I'll try to hum along,
And, maybe, sing again.

I hear the "healing" calling,
And I recognize the name.
The faces are all different,
But the "healing's" still the same.

I see the "healing" sobbing.
They need to know I care.
I must stop and comfort them,
And let them know I'm there.

I sense the "healing" being warned,
What their future holds in store.
I need to help them step by step,
'til they are whole once more.

I know the sounds of healing.
I've heard them all first hand.
You need to share your world with them,
For they don't understand

Yes! I know the sounds of "healing"
From others that I see.
God help me try to give to them,
What others gave to me.

CHAPTER TWENTY SEVEN

Roger, Tower

- My last neuropsychological battery of tests revealed I still had a rapid loss of information, severe attention problems, inability to distinquish essential information, difficulty staying on task, and problems with judgment. My scores in some of the attention subsections fell into the severely impaired range. But, I had a good retainment for overlearned information. So what else was new? I wish I had overlearned more information.

Dear God, It's me again.
Just one more thing, I guess.
Would you stay beside me
When I take my driving test?

I know I am more patient.
I want to pass, and yet,
Sometimes I know what I must do.
Sometimes I still forget.

I still want my dreams right now.
I'm trying to find the way.
It's hard to measure lifetimes,
When you live from day to day.

I still have my needs and wants,
For which I need to strive.
I'll give it everything that's in me,
If you'll only let me drive.

Like I learned, if I can try,
I know that I can do it.
It's not the motivation, Lord.
It's the paying attention to it.

So I know what's best for me,
And I can't keep it quiet.
I want to get behind the wheel,
And know that I will try it.

Roger, Tower

Please, God, don't rest just yet.
I need some other stuff.
Though I know I'll try my best,
It might not be enough.
I've relearned hands. I've relearned feet.
We've been through harder deals.
I know that I'm in search of wings,
But first, I need my wheels.
If both of us stay focused in,.
I'm sure that there's a way.
Please stay with me a moment more,
Until they say, "O.K."

Planning For The Future

Driving is my next goal. People with head injuries probably understand how I feel about driving. I need to feel my wings, to know I'm making progress. I'm headed in the right direction and getting there depends on how high I soar. I have all the fuel, I just need the tower's OK to turn the key and start the engine.

Driving is very important to me. It not only represents the ultimate freedom, but it will allow me to be independent, a privilege I so easily took for granted.

Most of my future plans depend on my ability to drive. I sit at home, and often think how selfish it is to want to drive so badly. How can I think of driving as such a high priority when there are many people who cannot walk? I know that what is a challenge to one is not for all; we each face our ultimate adversity, each of us on a different level. My worst fear has been I would not be able to drive. I don't think I will be able to cope with that very well. I've refused to believe other limitations and have beaten them. But the biggest step and accomplishment for me, will be returning independently to the road.

Although I am still highly distractible, New England Rehab apparently will refer me to a driving program for people who have disabilities like mine. Though they prefer not to, after much testing and much pleading, they will allow me the chance to fail. For the first time in over a year, I do not plan to accommodate them.

Kathy, my speech therapist, recommended that I hire a professional driver to relieve me of the pressure of needing to drive right away. She thinks that will be a help. It may solve a temporary problem, but it won't be a cure. I need to find a permanent cure and that is not to be satisfied with my becoming "Miss Daisy." I need and will, as always, DO IT MYSELF.

I need to be able to drive in order to resume my job as a real estate broker. I need to show and list properties, that requires being able to drive. I want to return to my job in real estate, if I can.

I need to be able to drive to continue as a gymnastics judge. I need to be able to travel to meets on my own. Sometimes I am the only one in my area assigned to judge. Gordon cannot be expected to drive me everywhere. He connects me to local rides, but even that is difficult when they occur daily and I don't get home until after 11 p.m. He has never complained, but it is not fair.

I need to drive to be able to help Gordon in our apartment business. I am no longer able to show or check out apartments, drop off receipts or answer tenant calls. It is hard on him to do his part of the business and then have to do most of mine. I am unable to collect rents or make bank deposits.

I know that I will make short work of the program for distractible drivers. Of course, I knew that I could walk safely a year ago too, when they confined me to a grey belt. I hope my insight and understanding of myself has improved since then. I know much time, effort and money has gone over the dam. Hopefully, it was worth it all.

At the time of this writing, I am waiting and hoping that those deficits that keep me from driving are lessened. We are concentrating specifically now on those at Rehab. The nurses still kid me and tell me I can't drive, I might end up in Minnesota. They may be right, but Minnesota's not all that bad. At least, I wouldn't have to check my luggage.

So I have decided that driving is my next attack. I never fail at what I strive to do and I try not to make excuses. I promise you, I will drive...that is a promise to me....that special kind of "down deep" promise that one never breaks.

CHAPTER TWENTY EIGHT

Reconnoitering

As you've probably deciphered by now, I have not slowed down much, nor do I intend to.

I am trying to accept myself as I am now. It is still hard. I think it always will be. There are times when I get very frustrated with myself and with others. Who doesn't? I have to try to remember to compensate for those things that create unusual problems because of my injury and accept others, that all people, without any injury have, as a normal part of life. Sometimes, it is extremely difficult to know the difference.

I have definitely had the hardest time coping with impatience, anger and fear. Those three still interfere with my gears. My husband has said he has had the most frustrating time dealing with my impatience. I want everything now, almost to a child-like need. Waiting for anything is very difficult for me. Waiting to do something is nearly impossible.

My handling of fear has totally reversed itself. Before my accident, I was a fighter when threatened. After my accident I resorted to "flight" instead. I ran from whatever was frightening. Now, I am learning to cope. Sometimes, I get overwhelmed and my behavior gets out of hand. I have come a long way in dealing with fear, and I think the feeling of being unable to exert any control is over.

I've also had to deal with an all consuming compulsion to make obscene hand gestures when suddenly angered. It had certainly not been a natural thing for me to even consider doing. This compulsion has occurred when I have been with colleagues and family. It has happened in traffic and when quick changes occur. I still have to deal with anger and confrontation. This is still a sensitive, frightening area for me. I have yet to recover the necessary coping skills. Much of my anger is still directed toward myself rather than a proper object. I know in theory what I have to do.

Considering how much I've improved and how many deficits I've learned to compensate for or overcome, I am really pleased with my rehabilitation and the job we've done.

I need the strength of my friends and colleagues, certainly not their sympathy. I have too much of my own sympathy.

I think, at long last, recovery and I are coming to grips with reality.

Part of me died this past year. I'm not sure if it's capable of being reborn. I still mourn for that part of me and that time.

It died somewhere in between the passing of a "time when" and the coming of a "time to."

For the first time ever, I found someone frightened and alone on the curb, afraid to step into the street. A parade had passed by. I had only a deflated balloon in my hand to know that it happened. I never heard the music of trumpets nor saw the colors of *Old Glory* as she passed.

I didn't know the end of my life's parade was coming. No one warned me, no one told me to watch out.

That *Old ME* just disappeared and marched off into the sunset with the rest of the bands.

Somewhere I know that parade is still moving onward down some street, carrying part of me away with it. I am still making as much noise, banging the drum, blowing my horn and waving the flag.

But as the sound of the band grows dimmer, ever softer, in the distance, I regret that people will never know the part of me that passed away with it and... disappeared forever.

ENDANGERED SPECIES

Bald eagles gliding in the sky,
Humpback whales within the sea,
Snow leopards in the cold wind,
                    ...and me.

Whooping cranes in nesting,
Herds of bison roaming free,
Desert tortoises in the sand,
                    ...and me.

Caribou among the winter pine,
The swallowtail on the tree,
Brown pelicans in the summer sun,
                    ...and me.

American crocodiles in the marsh,
Giant otters bask with glee,
Kangaroo rats out in the field,
                    ...and me.

Utah prairie dogs in the grass,
Orangutans, funny as can be,
Fishers in the forest wood,
                    ...and me.

Giant pandas playing house,
Brain coral from the sea,
Grey wolves nightly on the prowl,
                    ...and me.

You must look to find the Darter
and Great Horned Owl in the tree,
You had to search to find them
                    ...and me.

You recognized the Condor,
Grizzly Bear and Manatee,
But one died out unnoticed
                    ...me.

 # *Flaps Up!*

I have made some adjustments in my life now, in order to counteract the losses.

I try to remember to bring my leg brace (AFO), I still need it when my leg tires. If I forget, I put myself in danger of injury.

I take my husband with me whenever I can, I never tire of needing him. He is as much a source of my strength as I am to myself, and I wouldn't change that for anything.

I know I need to carry my memory book at all times. It has become my brain. Without it, I suffer badly from C.R.S. (Can't Remember Shit) and apparently will continue to forever. I don't accept this as an undeniable truth yet, but I'm very close.

I laugh at the good times. I still forget where I put things. When I can't find the iron, I now look behind the milk in the refrigerator. Chances are, it's there. My family is used to unleavened bread for lack of an ingredient, but it tastes OK. By showing up at places and forgetting why, I've managed to open new doors and new opportunities. I am too busy to waste time worrying about the unknown. I need to keep moving.

Many people ask me what has been the hardest thing for me. I could not have answered before. The fact that I can now, is a credit to my rehabilitation and indicative of my improvement.

It's acceptance, I will never again be the same person I was before my accident. It's too bad, because I really loved that person. I remember who she was, the things she was able to do and how fast she did them. She left during the parade. Of all the things I can't remember, I wish she was one of them.

It would make it easier to accept what's left.

I recently saw the movie *Regarding Henry*. Henry was lucky. He preferred himself as he was after his head injury rather than the person he was before the accident. If I just felt that same way, this change would be so much easier to handle.

I still have a very hard time accepting that new being within me. She is slow and different. I want to get away from her, but she is part of me. I am incapable of victory and unwilling to accept defeat. She is not the real ME I worked hard to become, and remember from yesterday.

She appeared in a fraction of a moment and took over my life. I have beaten her so far in everything I've undertaken. But she is still there, stumbling in her own mistakes.

She's still struggling to watch the traffic lights in order to step off the curb. She missed a part of life's parade but in the remnants, in the poetry, it is preserved.

She is still there. Sometimes, she cries too much. Sometimes, she doesn't know how. Sometimes, she tries too much. Sometimes, she doesn't know how.

I expose her in *From the Inside Out*. I want others to know the anger, the fear and hurt of head injury. I can say and write about many parts of me, but that is the hardest to share...that overnight transition that changed me into someone I didn't know and don't want to know.

Head injury is instantaneous. There is no time to adjust. There is no time to become accustomed to the slowness, the inabilities, the wanderings. If we are left with enough awareness to know and remember, it still hurts. It hurts very much. It hurts from the inside out.

FROM THE INSIDE OUT

I'VE HAD A HEAD INJURY...Pass the potatoes please?

I remember seeing, better than I remember hearing... So I look at my ingredients over and over. I need a record of the recipe. Without a recipe, I can't be put back together.

A stranger is living in me. I'm no longer what I was, or who I was, or who I want to be.

We have to travel together now, against my will. She's SO slow, I get impatient, but I need to "pick apart" her brain.

Yesterday's memories are stored away somewhere, needing and waiting to be rediscovered. But the attic door is locked from the inside. I'm still here but I can't get upstairs.

Time passes quickly for me, sometimes before it even happens. Someone said, "Nothing remembered is nothing lost." The memory book keeps the stranger within, contented and quiet.

I fight the struggles and failures. They belong to the stranger, but I am responsible. I forge the battle. I bare the wounds. But the stranger wins the war.

I cry out at night, but no one hears the screams. The stranger is asleep.

And during the day, I forget the night.

I try over and over again, but nothing works the way it was designed to, or I expect it to, or others want it to.

I crumble under stress, but it's NOT ME that's falling. I already ran away somewhere, and only my body is left here. My mind already escaped.

In times of fear, it IS ME panicking. My mind knows danger, but can't escape. My body already ran away and I don't know where its wandering. 9-1-1

And during the night, I forget the day.

Time passes slowly too, and sometimes time doesn't exist. Days pass unknowing and quickly come again to be reborn.... their prior birth, a stranger to me.

Flaps Up!

I want to do...to go...to be...to give. But the stranger needs to learn...to play ...to love...to live. I want to fly. She needs to crawl. I want a share. She gets it all.

I think I KNOW. (sometimes not enough) I know I THINK. (sometimes not enough) It's more often that I know I don't think, than I think I don't know. I'm not sure yet, if that's a help or a hindrance. The stranger doesn't like decisions.

When I am among a lot of people, she yearns for solitude. When I am alone, she needs the stimulation of people. This stranger and I have different needs.

My family loves me for what I was, and protects what I am. My friends cherish what I was, and often forget what I am. I remember who I was. I want to find out who I am. It's now 10 o'clock. At least I know where I am.

Laughter allows me to accept that I'm no longer the original. Crying keeps me aware that "Reality is never as good as the original dream."

I DO know the necessity of the universe to my life. I DON'T know the importance of my life to the universe. In fact, how to stay focused on anything is a real bummer.

I'm not a phoenix. This "falling and rising again from the ashes" is for the birds. But it breeds repetition and the stranger needs strategies. Strategies allow survival, and we are burning up at both ends.

Death is a one way ticket home. You only need money to buy it, the will to validate it, and a final destination. Its cheaper, but I don't think the stranger would even know how or where to get off.

Rehab is a round trip ticket to somewhere. It costs more, takes longer, and uses a lot more energy. The value is all "in the mind of the ticket holder". The final destination might even be a return to the attic.

I wonder why I wander. "Curiosity killed the cat." That cat obviously didn't look both ways before crossing the street. You should always check the lights first, before you step off the curb.

If you find ME out there somewhere, please check the traffic lights and send me home as soon as possible. A stamped, self-addressed envelope is enclosed for your convenience.

I HAVE A HEAD INJURY. Would you pass the potatoes, please? I don't understand. I don't even like potatoes. I never did.
Maybe they're for the stranger.

CHAPTER THIRTY

Toward the Unknown

I am charting my flight toward the unknown. I've come to realize many important truths during my search for wings.

Dreams begin when people say you can't. That's the time to climb into the cockpit. If you put every tear you shed feeling sorry for yourself into your fuel tank, you'll have enough power to keep flying forever.

Do not chart your journey with straight lines. It may be the shortest distance between here and there, but it won't be as exciting. The more often you stray off the path, the more fun you will have finding your way back.

In Search of Wings

As the saying goes, "If it feels good, do it."

Don't get bogged down with excuses and reasons why you shouldn't. There is something wonderful about walking right into life and doing the things you always dreamed about. If you think you can't, you'll be surprised when you do.

Don't put off your dreams until tomorrow. Tomorrows are made of too many "I wish" and "if onlys." Do things now before you forget and it is too late. Take time to say "hi" and "I love you." Hug each other and hold your friendships close. Cherish each moment. Your parade happens only once, and it is gone. You have to make sure it doesn't pass you by.

Don't keep your journey a secret. Encourage others to go with you and share your flight. While they will see things from their perspective, it will allow you to expand your own horizon.

Remember an eagle is an eagle wherever it flies. No one can make you less or diminish your value, unless you allow them to.

If you see someone else who is hurting, step forward and give them your hand. No one will be able to soothe them more than those who have found their wings and are, already soaring again. Take time to live, love, laugh, and pray.

Time does not heal all things. But many things will improve if left alone. Never leave head injury alone. We may not be healed by tomorrow, but with your help, we can make sure we are better than yesterday.

There are problems that still need answers. One of them is the fact that I appear perfectly normal. Most people who have sustained a head injury are not physically distinguishable. Perhaps that's good, but perhaps not. We share a common thread that makes us special. While we may operate at different levels of functioning, we are all slower than before. We have trouble concentrating and get over-stimulated easily. We need a little more rest than others. We must find time to get away and then we can come back stronger. We have to listen a little harder and we think a little slower. We may need to ask for repetition and make our own reminders.

We are very different from what we were before. Sometimes, only we ourselves know how different. We have to live with that knowledge forever. We are all learning daily how to live with ourselves. We know best what we need. We occasionally want help like everyone else, but we need to be allowed to try to succeed on our own and permitted to fail.

We are survivors. No one can appreciate survival without experiencing both ends of the success/failure spectrum. We, as survivors, have run the spectrum and know the way.

We have risen from the ashes and are prepared to continue our flight. We have already battled failure and have survived its wrath.

Taking off is usually an easy flight path. Most people travel down the paved runway and rise with the crowds. Because of our head injury, we are forced to rebuild the flight path and rise up alone. We need professionals to help us rebuild the runway. The trek itself, in search of wings, can only be taken by the survivor.

In the end I am taking the responsibility for myself. I am living my own life and trying to make my own decisions.

I am charting and following my own dreams. I still have them, you know. Although I may never be what I was before, I'm still trying to learn how to deal with the way I am.

Like other survivors, I am just another head injury statistic. But once I begin to soar again, no one will be able to quiet the sound of my wings. I want others to know the remnants of head injury, with all its hopes and dreams, hurt and scars, and memories of both.

And when the tears, fears, sadness, and anger have worn away, and the only parts left are the hopes and dreams, I will know that it has been for a good cause. At least I will feel relieved, knowing that I kicked and fought every inch of the way...that I never lacked for motivation. That often, without thinking, I stepped off that curb.

But I survived. I did what needed to be done. It may have scared the living daylights out of those watching, but I did it with no regrets. Part of me may have missed the parade, but the other part is overflowing with music.

I'm a survivor with a quest. My rehabilitation has been the journey. Quests are what dreams are made of and journeys are reality. I intend to follow my quest and continue the journey until the stranger and I are one again.

I will not allow myself to become another "dreamer" who had the ability to fly, but never left the ground. I plan to soar into the heavens and maybe even higher. For I intend to rise above all obstacles that impede my search for wings.

When people tell me that is impossible and I am just a person with a head injury, I answer them with my own strategies of repetition.

Nothing stops the human spirit
when it decides to soar.
It just needs the time to rest
and space to fly once more.

I have already taken the time to rest and, with more than enough help from my friends, found the space to fly again. Maybe, not all the way into the heavens yet but, at least, above the clouds, where others can not go...

.......without their wings........

Acknowledgments

Peter Raymond, of Picture This, Kennebunkport, Maine for his willingness to provide and permission to use his personal photographs. Included were the following: *Frequent Fliers* (pg. 39), *Reflection Of An Image* (pg. 46), *Without Fanfare* (pg. 63), *Disappearing* (pg. 136), *Priceless* (pg. 123), *Responsibility* (pg. 1);

Julie Motherwell, of Graphic Arts Consulting Services, Falmouth, Maine, for her help, guidance and professional knowledge;

Carrie and Kim: My daughters for their love during the hardest days of my life;

Elizabeth Pollack, Author, for her suggestions and sharing her knowledge with a novice;

Pat Zeitlin, my dear Friend for giving more than receiving and never caring;

Paule French, of Portland, Maine, for permission to use her photograph for the cover.

and most important of all to:

All of the survivors of head injury in the world that live my story every day.